STEP-BY-STEP GARDEN GUIDES

Werner M. Busch

Bonsai

AURA

Step-by-Step Garden Guides

Bonsai

Werner M. Busch

German-language edition and photographs
Gärtnern leicht und richtig Bonsai
© 1995 BLV Verlagsgesellschaft mbH, München

English-language edition
© 1996 Transedition Ltd, Oxford OX4 4DJ, England

Translation:
Andrew Shackleton/Asgard Publishing Services
Editing:
Asgard Publishing Services, Leeds
Typesetting:
Organ Graphic, Abingdon

This edition published in 2000
by **Aura Books**

10 9 8 7 6
Printed in Dubai

ISBN 0 947793 12 7

Growers' and collectors' credits

Nikos Amanatidis 15, 78, 79, 94/95; G. Arnold 55; Wolfgang Böttcher 46/47, 68/69; Hannelore Bünger 81; Bastian Busch 70/71; Johannes Caspary 9; Joe Genz 82/83; Dieter Hamacher 52/53; Reginald Jooren 64/65; Petra Niessen 17; M. Offermann 75; Walter Pall 72/73; Edith Reigber 63; Dieter Schmidt 48/49; Guido Sinn 70/71; Burghard Stirnberg 7; F.-J. Thönnessen 4/5, 56, 59; Werner Trachsel 41; Karl-Heinz Werner 60/61; Wolfgang Wirth 43.

Photographic credits

All photos from Meyer-Horn except pages 13 (Bonsai Club of Germany), 21 (Noel Whittall).

An eight-year-old Japanese white pine on a rock

CONTENTS

What is bonsai?

Many different things are under-
stood by the term 'bonsai', but
strictly speaking, according to
the oriental tradition, bonsai is
an art form in which a small but
mature tree is transformed by
human intervention so that it
complements its container and
recreates, in miniature, the
appearance of a mature tree in
the wild.

There are various ways of
achieving this — for instance,
by pruning the branches in a
particular way. And just as the
appearance of trees in the wild
will vary in different regions of
the world, so bonsai in different
countries can be adapted so that
they conform to characteristic
local growth patterns.

The equivalent Chinese term
for these miniature trees is
penjin. According to the much
older Chinese tradition the tree
is allowed to grow more freely,
and can even be permitted to
adopt a very eccentric growth
habit. In Japan, however, the
various styles of bonsai are
subject to strict rules that have
to be carefully observed; bonsai
trees are even categorised
according to size.

The great majority of Western
growers have followed the
Japanese tradition (the word
'bonsai' comes from Japanese).
So although this miniature art
form originated in China,

Western knowledge of the subject comes mainly from Japan, and Western methods are much closer to the Japanese than the Chinese tradition. Western growers will therefore generally adopt the Japanese styles, and these in turn provide the most useful models for beginners to follow.

Bonsai, just like painting, sculpture or even poetry, can only become a true art form when you have perfected the various practical skills, and developed the necessary creative and artistic sensibilities. But bonsai, unlike other art forms, is never finished, because the plants continue to grow.

Why take up bonsai?

Perhaps, as with most people, your interest in bonsai has arisen from a love of things oriental. However, other factors will come into play as you become better acquainted with the subject.

Working with trees can be a satisfying activity in itself, because bonsai brings you closer to trees than perhaps any other horticultural discipline. It encourages you to observe nature more closely, learning to recognise the tree species that

Autumn colours highlight the beauty of this 30-year-old trident maple.

occur in your area and watching how they grow in the wild. This, in turn, can provide deep insights into the laws of nature and the ways in which trees function as plants.

Trees have great symbolic significance in many oriental cultures, but this significance is not confined to the East. In the West, too, trees have strong associations with ancient mythology, and this can make them even more fascinating to work with.

Most people who take up bonsai are drawn to it mainly by the creative aspects of the subject — the idea of taking a tree and moulding it to suit your own imagination, using carefully laid-down procedures. In this way you can give expression to your own feelings about nature. Your bonsai can, for example, express a sense of struggle or a sense of harmony — or it can give an impression of lush growth or of maturity.

On the other hand, buying bonsai can also be a way of channelling the collector's urge until, with time, every inch of your garden, patio or windowsill is occupied by bonsai. If you reach this stage, you would be wise to consider whether you can really do justice to all the plants in your care. After your first buying binge, it may perhaps be more sensible to give some of your bonsai away so that you can concentrate on keeping just a few plants in the healthiest and most attractive style possible.

The main elements

The best way to assess the quality of a particular bonsai display is to look at each of the main elements that work together to create the final effect. These elements are: the container, the soil surface, the root spread, the trunk, the branches, the leaves, the flowers and finally the fruit.

The bonsai container
The bonsai container and the tree should form a single, harmonious whole. For instance, the container should be proportionate in size to the crown, its shape should suit that of the tree, and the glazed surfaces should not be conspicuous.

Here are a few simple rules to help you choose the right container:

- You cannot expect a bonsai and its container to complement one another properly until the bonsai is fully mature. So while a plant is in the early stages of its growth, keep it in a comparatively large container that has as simple a design as possible. The bonsai will develop faster in this kind of environment.

- In a fully developed bonsai, the depth of the container should equal the width of the base of the trunk. One notable exception to this is the cascade-style bonsai, which should always be placed in a much deeper container.

- The container should be shaped so that the rim lies more or less beneath the outer edge of the crown, and the diameter of the container should be less than the height of the tree — ideally, in fact, it should be about two-thirds the the height of the tree.

- The colours and patterns in the glaze should either be repeated in the colours of the tree, or at the very least match those of the tree.

- Choose a round or oval container for a tree with soft outlines, and a rectangular container for a tree with a more sharply defined habit.

The soil surface
The soil surface should be covered with thin but continuous patches of moss. If you want to leave any weeds, you should limit them to specific areas of the soil. Closely related to the mosses are the liverworts, which spread out more sparsely. Remove these — they will stop the soil from breathing.

Moss will only develop properly if you keep your bonsai out in the open; the air indoors is usually too dry. If you need to keep a plant indoors, then you'll have to resort to moss-like substitutes such as baby's tears (*Soleirolia*), *Selaginella*, small ferns or various clover species (*Trifolium*).

The root spread
The point where the roots connect to the trunk is very important, because this is what chiefly determines how old the tree appears to be. A tree will look really mature if it has strong, visible roots that spread out in all directions — although they should not be allowed to become *too* horizontal.

Young plants have a poorly developed root structure, and will need to be modified by careful, regular pruning. When pruning the roots, cut out all the vertical roots growing below the trunk, and leave just the side roots. These will then develop more strongly in order to supply

Strong roots should be visible at the base of the trunk.

the tree with nutrients, and this will produce the appropriate root spread.

The trunk

The trunk is the most important element in bonsai: it will be the basis for the tree's character and development.

The trunk should be as thick as possible at the base and taper gently upwards towards the top of the tree. It is best to avoid sudden changes in the girth of the trunk (though sometimes, admittedly, it can be hard to prevent them).

The best way to create a nicely tapering trunk is to cut back the main trunk repeatedly during the early stages of growth, meanwhile allowing one of the side branches to grow taller so it can take over the role of the trunk. This drastic pruning measure will also determine the eventual shape and direction of the trunk.

The branches

The eventual size, shape and direction of the branches should be such that they emphasise the characteristics of the trunk. If the trunk is straight, then the branches should be straight, too. If the trunk has a slight curve, then the branches should be similarly curved.

The thickness of the branches must also appear natural. If the trunk is thick, then thin branches will look immature. Horizontal or drooping branches give an impression of great age. It's also important for the branches to be be thicker towards the bottom of the tree and become progressively thinner towards the top.

A well-developed branch is thickest at its base (where it joins the trunk) and tapers outwards, dividing into a fine structure of twigs. You can create such a shape by pruning the branches regularly. Each pruning will change the direction of growth. On a well-formed branch, the distance between each change of direction should become progressively shorter as you move outward towards the tip.

A larch in its autumn colours

The leaf on the right is from a wild elm tree; the one on the left came from a bonsai of the same species.

The leaves

The leaves should be as small as possible in proportion to the size of the bonsai. Having said that, the ratio between the two cannot be anywhere near the same as for a tree in the wild.

Bonsai growers generally choose trees whose leaves are naturally small. Shrubs tend to have much smaller leaves than full-size trees — after all, very few full-size trees have really small leaves.

With bonsai, however, there are some specific ways of limiting the size of the leaf to as little as one-third of its natural size in the wild. The principle that you need to follow is fairly simple: the more finely the branches divide, the smaller the leaves will be. Each time you prune, you will create ever more finely divided branches — so the more you prune, the smaller the leaves should eventually become.

Cutting the leaves themselves will also help to fill out the crown. Cut some or all of the leaves back so that only the leaf stems remain. Soon each of the tiny buds along the stem will sprout again, and the stem itself will grow into a twig. After only a few weeks each of the original leaves will develop into a new branch — and each of these branches will be covered with small leaves.

Since leaf cutting sharply reduces the reserves available to the tree, you can't expect any of the main branches to grow thicker at the same time. It's best to wait until the tree has matured before you do any leaf cutting. It is, after all, much more important for young trees to develop strong branches, so it's really best to ensure that you don't cut their leaves in these early stages.

The flowers

Even on an individual plant, flowering behaviour will vary enormously from year to year. Flowering also depends on the species, the age of the plant and its state of health — and it is further influenced by the weather conditions, the temperature of the soil, and the amount of water and nutrients that are stored in the soil.

Generally speaking, bonsai flowers are no smaller than their wild equivalent, so they will inevitably be out of proportion with the plant. This means that if you want to grow bonsai for their flowers, you should always choose varieties that naturally develop small flowers.

Some trees, such as elm and beech, have rather insignificant flowers with little creative or decorative value. Others, however, are grown specifically for their attractive blossoms. These include the pomegranate and crab apple, and shrubs such as the azalea.

Even in these cases, flowering should take a back seat during the initial development phase, when you should be concentrating on creating the right growth habit. It simply is not possible to produce really good flowers *and* a really good growth habit at one and the same time. If you want to do that, you will be forced to make compromises. With the pomegranate, for example, you will have to accept over-long shoots, as the flower will only appear at the very end of a shoot.

Flowering behaviour will also be influenced by other factors such as how you fertilise your plants. This will include both the timing of feeds and the types of fertiliser that you use.

The fruits

The fruits can make a bonsai extremely valuable, and they also make for variety in its appearance.

However, fruiting uses up a lot of the plant's energy, so you should only leave fruits on a plant if they have some decorative value. Berry fruits, for example, can be left on the tree. Crab apples, on the other hand, drop their fruit if they become too heavy.

Artistically it's all a matter of proportion. If the fruits are insignificant (as they are on azaleas, for instance), or if, like quinces, they are too heavy, then some of them at least should be removed — and while a tree is still developing, it's better to remove *all* the fruit. Heavily fruiting trees will not grow very much, and the branches will not be able to thicken up at all.

This 15-year-old crab apple is laden with fruit.

The Japanese styles

A bonsai is supposed to look like an old tree, albeit one in miniature form.

With regular pruning it is easy enough to create a miniature form, but creating the appearance of an old tree is rather more of a challenge. To succeed in this, you will need to begin by looking at the growth habits of old trees in the wild, and learning to recognise their characteristics.

The Japanese have been doing this for many centuries, and they have used their observations to develop a whole series of stylised growth habits. This was how the various Japanese bonsai styles evolved, and these in turn were grouped into various categories on the basis of common characteristics.

A knowledge of the various Japanese styles is extremely helpful, not only when you are creating your own bonsai, but also when you are buying bonsai or visiting a bonsai exhibition.

Upright style

In the upright style, the trunk forms the main axis from the root right up to the tip of the tree. If you look at the tree from the front, the branches should fork alternately to the left and to the right. No two branches should emerge from the same point on the trunk. In the top third of the tree, and only in the

top third, there may be branches growing forwards. At the back, the crown can be allowed to fill out rather more. All the branches should be mainly horizontal or slightly drooping.

The **formal upright style** (below) is characterised by a tall, straight trunk; in the **informal upright style** (above) the trunk is allowed to twist and

turn a little, sometimes in the form of S-bends. The branches should always emerge from the outside of a bend. The upright style is particularly suited to conifers, but foliage trees, too, are often shaped to this style.

Broom style

In broom-style bonsai (below) the trunk does not run in a straight line from root to tip. Instead of this, it divides at a certain point into three or more branches of roughly equal dimensions, which should all grow diagonally upwards so as to form a broad crown. The broom style is almost entirely limited to foliage trees.

At the front you should be able to glimpse the main branches through the foliage. When the crown is covered with leaves, it should usually be round, oval or umbrella-shaped, and the supporting trunk should not be too long. The structure of the branches should be visible only in winter, when the leaves have fallen.

Raft style

In the raft style (below) a line of trunks emerges from a single large trunk, only part of which is visible above the soil surface. Such forms occur naturally when a large tree is overturned in bad weather but is not uprooted. The branches, which have now become upright, develop into a line of independent trees, often with separate individual crowns.

Slanting style

In this case the trunk should be growing more or less at an angle. The style will look natural only if the roots are well spread out, despite the angle of the trunk. The main branches should be horizontal or slightly drooping.

Twin trunks

In a twin-trunk bonsai two (mainly upright) trunks emerge from the same roots. One trunk should be noticeably taller and thicker than the other, but the two should form a single crown.

Windswept style

Here the trunk is once again set at an angle, while the branches all grow in the same direction as the slant of the trunk. Trees shaped like this occur naturally along windswept coasts, where the whole tree seems to lean away from the prevailing winds.

Multiple trunks

A multiple-trunk bonsai should have three or more trunks growing from the same roots. According to tradition, there should be an odd number of trunks. They should vary in height and girth, but the tree will look more natural if the taller trunks are also the thickest. Again, the trunks should form a single, composite crown.

Group planting

In this case (see illustration overleaf) a whole group of single trees is planted in a large, flat container to create a kind of miniature forest.

The trees should vary in size, but the taller ones should also be thicker so as to create the impression that the trees are of different ages.

This style will look natural only if trees are planted at randomly spaced intervals, and not arranged in rows. The trees should not be allowed to hide each other when viewed from the front; this makes it possible

11

to look right into the 'forest'. At the back, however, they should be left to grow together. If you place most of the shorter, thinner trees at the back and the taller, thicker ones at the front, this will make the 'forest' seem much deeper.

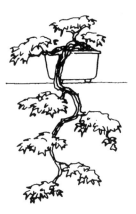

Cascade style

This style is unusual in that the tip of the trunk is no longer the highest point of the tree, and is usually hanging down. In the full cascade style (see above), the tip of the trunk is in fact lower than the bottom of the container.

The container used for the cascade style is also unusual in being much deeper than a conventional bonsai container. This is necessary as much for stability as for the general appearance of the display.

The cascade style has a number of interesting variants. Most of these imitate tree shapes that occur naturally, such as on overhanging cliffs, or on steep mountain slopes where they are subject to high winds and heavy winter snows.

Planting on a rock

There are two very distinct styles for planting bonsai on a rock, commonly known in English as clasped-to-rock and root-over-rock styles.

Clasped-to-rock style

In this style (shown below) quite a small tree is planted on a relatively large, porous rock. The roots are set in a depression or hole in the rock. The rock stands in a container full of water, which is drawn up through the rock by capillary

action. The water eventually reaches the hole where the tree is planted, and can then be absorbed by the plant.

Root-over-rock style

Here the roots of the tree grow over a relatively small rock, and are in direct contact with the soil beneath. This style of tree can be kept in an ordinary bonsai container.

Literati or *bunjin* style

This is a very unusual style (see above). The tree has a very long, slender and interestingly shaped trunk that carries only a few branches. This style is often said to have been inspired by the elaborate characters of Japanese script. But this seems unlikely, as the term *bunjin* derives from an old Chinese word *wenjen*, which referred to the literati or educated classes. Perhaps a more likely source of inspiration were the tall, spindly but graceful trees portrayed in Chinese paintings.

A 12-year-old birch — height about 30 in (80 cm)

The traditional Japanese styles can be a great help in creating your own bonsai. You will often have to make compromises because of a plant's individual characteristics, but don't be discouraged. Just remember that even when the results you achieve are less than perfect, they will often have a beauty that is all their own.

The right environment

When you're looking for the right place to keep a particular bonsai, start by thinking about the country where the species originated. Bonsai plants can be divided into three main categories on this basis.

Firstly, there are those plants that will grow out of doors throughout the year. These include the majority of western European and North American species, and most of the bonsai imported from Japan.

This small-leaved lime has grown to just 20 in (50 cm) in 13 years.

For at least part of the year, plants in the other two groups will need more warmth than they will generally get out of doors in Britain.

The first of these two groups consists of the so-called cool-greenhouse plants. These plants should be kept cool but frost-free through the winter. Most of them come from regions with either a Mediterranean-type or a subtropical climate.

The other group includes the various tropical plants, which can only thrive in a warm greenhouse or in a room with equivalent conditions.

Outdoor bonsai

Outdoor (as opposed to indoor) bonsai are created from species that are native to regions with a cool-temperate climate, much like ours in Britain.

Our outdoor temperatures and humidity levels should be just about right for these plants. However, they'll need plenty of sunshine and constant breezes; for if you grow them in too sheltered an environment, this will make them less resistant to pests. Outdoor bonsai, especially if they have plenty of leaves, are liable to be occupied, sucked and eaten by the same insects and other pests that afflict their wild cousins in the surrounding countryside.

However, as long as they are well cared for — and as long as they've adapted to the outdoor climate — such bonsai can deal with most pests without human intervention. Admittedly this doesn't apply to certain persistent pests such as the ubiquitous red spider mite.

Some outdoor bonsai, such as oaks or pines, can stand out in the sun all day. Others, like beeches and azaleas, prefer a more shaded position.

Indoor bonsai

You need to bear in mind that in their native countries, the plants we keep indoors will normally live out of doors. Unfortunately, our indoor climate is different in most respects from that of their tropical homes. Only the temperatures

A ten-year-old pomegranate bearing just one fruit

are likely to be similar — and only figs (*Ficus*) and a few other succulents will readily adapt to normal indoor conditions. Most tropical plants need higher humidity levels — and more light and ventilation — than can normally be made available to them indoors.

However, you can modify these factors to improve growing conditions for your bonsai. For instance, you can increase humidity levels by placing your containers on a large tray filled with gravel or with hydroponic granules. Keep it topped up with water, but never allow the containers to come directly into contact with the water, as this will make the soil inside them too wet. The water will evaporate in the warm room, ensuring that the air around the plants is always humid.

The behaviour of a plant will tell you if it needs more light. If the leaves on new shoots are more widely spaced than on the branches that were there when you bought the plant, then it clearly needs more light. If you can't find a better-lit position, then you will need special plant lamps to make up the shortfall. These lamps produce light at the right wavelengths for the plant to absorb and utilise it.

Some trees — pomegranates and sageretias, for example — tend to produce foliage that is too tender when they're kept indoors. The best solution in this case is to install a fan nearby to keep the air circulating around them. Use a time switch so that it will come on for just a few hours each day.

Warm-greenhouse plants can be kept in the same conditions all year round, but those suited to a cool greenhouse should be kept in an unheated room during the winter. They are usually comfortable as long as the temperature remains below 64°F (18°C), and will even survive temperatures close to freezing point (32°F; 0°C).

All indoor bonsai can be placed out in the garden during the summer. But you must give them the chance to adapt gradually to direct sunlight, or else the leaves can easily become scorched.

15

Watering

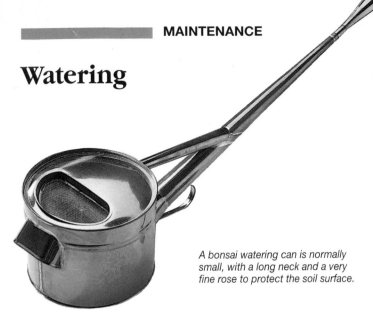

A bonsai watering can is normally small, with a long neck and a very fine rose to protect the soil surface.

The simplest rule for watering is this: when the surface of the soil is dry to touch, it's time for you to water the tree.

For most species it doesn't really matter what method you use, so you can simply do it the way that you find easiest. Either plunge the container briefly into water, or water your bonsai exactly as you would water any other plant.

Plunging the container into water will saturate the roots, which will then stay wet for longer. On the other hand, if your bonsai has recently been repotted, or if the container is unusually deep, then it's better to water it from above. This will help to prevent the soil staying wet for too long, which can starve the roots of oxygen.

Water is essential to a plant in a number of different ways. As well as supplying certain nutrients to the plant, it acts as a transport medium, carrying salts from the roots to the leaves, and sugars from the leaves down to the roots. It also helps to stabilise the cells of the plant by building up their internal pressure, and enables the plant to cool through the process of transpiration.

The roots will only absorb water if concentrations of salt inside the plant are higher than those outside it. This is because water is attracted towards higher concentrations of salt — so plants enrich their cells with salts in order to draw up more water into themselves. The more salts the plant cells contain, compared to the surrounding soil, the more water they are going to absorb.

Conversely, the more salts there are in the soil, the more difficult it is for the plant to absorb enough water for its needs — especially since the plant cells cannot easily increase their concentrations of salt beyond a certain point.

The salt content of the soil is greatly affected by the quality of the water it receives. Water containing a high level of dissolved salts will naturally increase the salt concentrations in the soil. But even if the water has relatively few salts dissolved in it, their concentration will increase if the soil is exposed to direct sunlight — the water will evaporate, and the salts will be left behind.

To avoid the soil becoming too rich in salts, you should try to use water with a low concentration of them (i.e. less than 300 mg/l). Give your plants plenty of water at regular intervals, allowing most of it to drain off — this will help to flush out any excess salts.

Water supplies

Apart from distilled or de-ionised water, rain water is the lowest in salts. The concentration can be as little as 50–100 mg/l. Obviously this makes rain water the best solution, and you'll need to store plenty of it for use in hot weather.

Collecting and storing rain water is no problem if you've got a garden. If you only have a balcony available, you can run a pipe from a roof gutter and collect the rain water in a suitable butt. Systems like this should be easy to find at your local DIY or gardening centre, and they aren't particularly difficult to set up.

However, there will inevitably come a time — during a drought, for instance — when your supply of rain water is exhausted and you need to find an alternative source.

Spring water is extremely variable in the amount of salt it contains, which often changes even from season to season.

Tap water also varies depending on the source of supply, although in most places the salt content remains constant over the year. Hard water, even after it has been treated with a water softener, is generally very high in salts, while soft water is lower. Your local water company should hopefully be able to tell you how hard or soft their tap water is. Failing that, there are kits available for testing the hardness of your water.

You can reduce the salt content of hard water by boiling it (which removes carbonates), or even by allowing it to stand for a while. You can also mix hard water with soft water to reduce its salt concentration.

A 15-year-old crab apple in blossom

The soil

By comparison with other cultivated plants, bonsai are kept in an extremely small container. You will need to take this into account when deciding what soil mixture you want to use.

Trees don't like to stand in water, so the soil should be well drained to allow excess water to escape through the holes in the container. The soil composition should also have a stabilising effect. As a bonsai container holds only very small amounts of soil, any changes in the environment can produce substantial changes to its make-up. It's important to ensure that the soil composition is such that these wide swings can be evened out.

The pH value of the soil is very important for the welfare of the tree. The pH is a measure of the number of hydrogen (H^+) ions present in the soil. These in turn determine how many other ions are available to the plant. They also affect chemical processes, and influence the behaviour of micro-organisms in the soil. Soil with a low pH is called an *acid* soil; soil with a high pH is classed as *alkaline. Neutral* soil has a pH of around 7.

For a few plants, the exact pH value is crucial, but most will tolerate a fairly broad range of values. Most trees thrive in soil with a pH of 5-6. Exceptions to this will be clearly indicated in the chapters on individual tree species, where you'll also find information about soil mixtures most suitable for each of them.

Bonsai soil normally includes the following components:

Loam is capable of storing a lot of water, which is then only slowly absorbed by the tree. This means that the tree is not left standing in the water for a long time after watering, yet there is still plenty of water available to it in the short term.

Much the same applies to the salt content of the soil. After an application of mineral-rich fertiliser, the soil becomes enriched with salts. Loam absorbs most of the nutrient salts, and makes their ions available to the tree by exchanging them for the ions expelled by the roots. However, the loam retains larger amounts of phosphorus. When applying fertiliser to a soil that is rich in loam, make sure you choose a high-phosphorus fertiliser to compensate for this.

Loam is normally fine-textured, and loamy soil can quickly become compacted. So the best form for bonsai is a granular loam such as *akadama*, which retains its granular consistency for a long time. *Akadama*, however, is very expensive — it has to be imported from Japan. A cheaper British alternative is John Innes No 3.

The very best bonsai mixture includes the following (clockwise from top left): sand, lava granules, loam granules (akadama), fine gravel and planting compost. If the lava and loam granules are too expensive, then fine gravel and John Innes No 3 will do instead.

Peat consists mainly of organic material. It is chemically acid, and absorbs water extremely well. True peat is becoming more difficult to obtain, as available resources have become limited and further exploitation threatens our environment. However, a number of equally effective substitutes have now come onto the market.

Sand improves the porosity of peaty or loamy soils.

Planting compost is a compost that is poor in nutrients. It is usually a mixture of sand and peat, or peat substitutes. It provides for good porosity and good water storage at the same time, making it an ideal component for a bonsai mixture.

Fine gravel improves the soil's porosity and drainage capacity.

Lava granules improve ventilation, but can also store large amounts of water and increase the level of trace elements in the soil. But like *akadama* they are an expensive luxury; sand and fine gravel will also help to improve soil porosity.

Young plants will need new soil every year. Older bonsai plants need the soil to be changed every two to four years. The best time to do this is in spring.

This 15-year-old trident maple has grown to a height of just 20 in (50 cm).

19

Feeding and fertilisers

Feeding makes a great difference to the development of bonsai during the course of the year, so it's extremely important to choose the right fertilisers — the ones that will benefit your plant the most.

If you're a newcomer to bonsai, it's best to use an organic feed, as this is unlikely to cause damage if applied in excess.

Indoor bonsai will need feeding throughout the year, at varying intervals. Outdoor bonsai, on the other hand, will need feeding only during the main growth period.

Important nutrients

The most important nutrients required are nitrogen (N), phosphorus (P), potassium (K), magnesium (Mg) and various trace elements.

Nitrogen

This is needed for all the plant's growth processes. You can even control these processes by regulating the nitrogen supply. If there's plenty of nitrogen available, you can expect plenty of growth. Conversely, reducing the nitrogen will slow down the plant's growth.

If you provide large quantities of nitrogen, you should adjust the amount carefully in proportion to other nutrients, or the plant will lose its resistance to pests and diseases.

Phosphorus

This element plays an equally important part in harnessing the energy of the plant.

Remember that the more loam there is in the soil, the more phosphorus the fertiliser should contain. This is because loam absorbs a high proportion of the phosphorus and makes it unavailable to the plant.

Potassium

The third of the three main nutritional elements, potassium promotes the development of woody tissue, which in turn helps the plant to become more frost-hardy. Potassium also improves water uptake in the roots, making the plant more resistant to drought.

These two factors together mean that outdoor bonsai will need plenty of potassium in the summer and early autumn.

Magnesium

Magnesium is needed in smaller quantities than the first three elements, but plays a major role as one of the building blocks of chlorophyll. It is also vital to some of the chemical exchanges that take place within the plant. Conifers need more magnesium than broadleaves.

Trace elements

This category includes a series of vital plant nutrients that are needed only in tiny quantities.

More often than not, ample quantities of trace elements are already present in the soil. But if a tree stands in the same soil for several years, it will sometimes exhaust these supplies. So eventually you will need to provide additional trace elements to make up for the loss.

Adjusting to changing requirements

Over the course of a year, a plant will have very different nutrient requirements at different times.

When giving nutrients, it's important to keep the amounts correctly balanced with one another, though the exact quantities can vary — within certain limits. (In practice, for instance, a slow-release fertiliser such as Osmacote will cover most requirements for the spring and summer seasons.)

Fertiliser packets will usually indicate the percentages of nitrogen (N), phosphorus (P) and potassium (K) that they contain according to the simple formula NPK. From these percentages you can work out their relative proportions.

If, for example, the NPK values for a fertiliser are given as 10:5:5, this means it contains 10 percent of nitrogen, 5 percent of phosphorus and 5 percent of potassium — so the proportion of these nutrients relative to one another can be given as 2:1:1.

If a fourth value is given after the NPK values, it will refer to magnesium (Mg).

Nutrient requirements also vary between plants at different stages of growth. Young, developing plants, for example, need to grow vigorously from the first spring growth through to June, which means that during this period they need large and regular doseds of a high-nitrogen fertiliser (NPK values in the proportion 2:1:1).

After that, fertiliser amounts should remain the same, but they should contain a lower proportion of nitrogen (NPK values 1:1:1). Then, from August onwards, you will need to increase the amounts of potassium as autumn approaches: NPK values should then be in the proportion 1:2:3.

Plants in their first container will need a similar regime. Start the year with a weak feed in the proportion 2:1:1, and strengthen the feed with the first vigorous growth in the spring.

A mature bonsai should not grow as vigorously as a young or developing plant. Only the finer branches will be in need of improvement, and you can achieve this by pinching out the young shoots. This stops the spring growth in its tracks — after you've done it there will be only a little further growth, which means that the plant's requirement for nitrogen will be correspondingly low.

Such mature bonsai should be fed in moderate doses from the first spring growth right through to August, ideally with a feed whose NPK values are in the proportion 1:2:3.

A selection of bonsai fertilisers, all of them available in this country

 A proper supply of nutrients is vital for the health, growth and general development of all bonsai. Try to follow the instructions given under each plant described in this book. You can avoid overfeeding by applying fertilisers frequently but in small, carefully measured doses.

Pests and how to deal with them

All trees have evolved at much the same pace as the pests that infest them — that's how they have learned to live with them. Mature trees in the wild are therefore extremely unlikely to be killed by diseases or by the ravages of pests.

The same, alas, cannot be said for bonsai plants. These trees are so small that a whole plant can be picked bare by just a few caterpillars, while an infestation of red spider mites could quite easily kill off every single leaf on the tree.

Animal pests

Larger leaf-eating insects can easily be removed by hand. However, outdoor bonsai can only be protected effectively if the pests are dealt with at the beginning of the year, before they have a chance to attack the first young leaves.

You can kill off spider mites, lice and other arachnid or insect pests in their egg or larval forms by spraying them with an oil-based preparation. The oil doesn't poison them; it simply blocks the breathing pores of the eggs and larvae so that the tiny creatures are quickly suffocated.

If you use a systemic killer, containing both oil and a suitable insecticide, this will attack a whole spectrum of insect pests. The combination is highly effective. The oil enters hidden crevices and penetrates waterproof wax excretions; and this in turn brings the insecticide into direct contact with the pests in their egg or larval state, before they have a chance to emerge from the plant tissue where the adult insects have placed them.

Unfortunately these systemic insecticides are often highly poisonous, and — more importantly — they make no distinction between actual pests and the·various beneficial insects. The best time to use them is therefore between the swelling of the first buds and the appearance of the first green leaf tips. That way, the pests will not be attacked until the point where they finally emerge.

You should treat indoor bonsai just as soon as you see any pest or infestation. At this stage it should normally still be possible to remove the wretched little creatures by hand.

These three oak leaves have been attacked by (from bottom left) gall wasps, mildew and leaf miners.

Fungal diseases

Most of the various fungi that attack our native trees go through a dormant phase during the winter period. This applies, for example, to those fungi that later go on to inhabit the leaves, because they infect the fresh spring growth from the very moment it begins to emerge.

In the short time before they penetrate the leaves, these potentially dangerous fungi can be dealt with using a fungicidal spray. Apply it just as the first green tips emerge from the leaf buds. This procedure should prevent the plant from being infected with mildew, or with one of the various leaf-spot diseases.

To remove any traces of the fungi in their dormant stage, you should clear away all dead leaves — and cut out any dead branches to stop all the various fungi that attack the wood.

Once the fungi have invaded the tissue of the plant, they will be extremely difficult to eradicate. Often the only solution is to apply some kind of systemic fungicide after you have sprayed the plant.

Fungal infections are often a sign that a plant hasn't been properly looked after. If you plant your tree in the right soil mixture, keep it under the right conditions, and apply the correct quantities of water and nutrients, then the tree should be capable of warding off any infection by itself.

As for the correct treatment to use, it's best to ask an expert for advice. The various fungicides are constantly being replaced by new ones that require different application methods. If the chemical you're about to use is actually poisonous — or at the very least dangerous to health — then it's best to ask an expert to carry out the treatment.

Fungicides also have the same disadvantage as insecticides in that they kill off the beneficial fungi as well as the ones you are attempting to eradicate. So before applying any fungicide, you should always cover up the container completely. Otherwise the chemical may kill off various beneficial fungi in the soil, some of which the tree may even need in order to live. If you kill these off, then you may be killing off the tree as well.

Most woodland trees enjoy a symbiotic relationship with certain fungi — a relationship that benefits both parties.

 As long as your plants remain healthy enough, they will be able to ward off disease without the assistance of chemicals. Ideal conditions and careful maintenance are the best way of preventing such problems. Always keep your bonsai plants in the right conditions, feeding and watering them on a regular basis.

Bonsai tools

There is a wide range of specialist tools available to help you in the process of creating bonsai. Their various functions are briefly explained below (the numbers given in brackets correspond to those in the picture opposite):

Bonsai shears (12-14)
These are used to trim both the branches and the roots:

- The long-handled variety (12) is for thinning out a dense crown full of tiny branches.

- For thicker branches you will need much heftier shears (14) with handles designed to fit the whole hand.

Branch cutters (1-4)
These are designed to remove a whole branch or root and leave a wound that will heal quickly:

- Concave cutters (4) produce an oval-shaped wound that goes slightly into the wood; the cutting edges are slanted so as to help you reach awkward places.

- Knob cutters (1-2) produce a more circular wound that heals more quickly, although their shape means they can't always reach the places they're needed for.

- Spherical concave cutters (3) combine the best qualities of the other two types, but are also much more expensive.

Jinning pliers (6)
This tool is used for working on split branches — a process known as *jinning*. You pull off the bark and tear out some of the fibres to create what looks like a damaged branch on an ancient tree. Jinning pliers can also be very useful for bending thick pieces of wire into loops for securing tensioned wire.

Bonsai wire cutters (5)
These cutters are specially designed for removing wire from branches where it has become too tight. They are shaped so that you can cut wires close to the branch without damaging the bark.

Root hook (8)
This very simple device is very useful when repotting a plant and trimming the roots. You can use it to loosen and disentangle the roots. You can also use it to reveal the root spread if it is hidden under the soil.

Bonsai brush (10)
You'll need this for working on the soil surface after a plant has been repotted. It can be used to expose the root spread and to remove rough material from the soil surface.

Tweezers (7)
These are ideal for removing unwanted weeds and liverwort from the soil. They sometimes have a spade-like tip for pressing down the soil afterwards. This tool can also be used for pinching out fresh shoot tips to stop further growth.

Leaf-cutting scissors (15)
These are used for cutting leaves to encourage branching (see page 8). They are designed to spring open again after every cut, so that only a single movement is needed each time.

Brushes (9)
These come in various degrees of stiffness. They are useful for working on the trunk, and for removing algae and rotting tissues after jinning (see above). They can also be used if the soil around the root spread is too hard for a standard bonsai brush to remove.

Bending jack (11)
This very special tool is used to change the shape and direction of a thick trunk. It's covered with rubber tubing to prevent any pressure marks being left on the trunk.

 Don't buy a lot of specialist tools when you're just starting out. With a little imagination you can carry out the vast majority of essential tasks using ordinary gardening equipment. The first specialist tools you are likely to need are bonsai shears, a concave branch cutter and a knob cutter.

The cutting tools are made from a variety of different metals. If they are black, then they are probably made of ordinary steel. These are the cheapest tools, but they're also liable to rust if they come into contact with water, so it's always a good idea to oil them lightly when you've finished using them.

If you want to avoid rust, you can buy tools made of chrome or stainless steel. However, they are much more expensive than tools made of ordinary steel, and may not necessarily be a better buy. You'll find that most cutting tools will have a similar lifespan, whatever metal they are made from.

A selection of bonsai tools (the numbers refer to those given in brackets in the text)

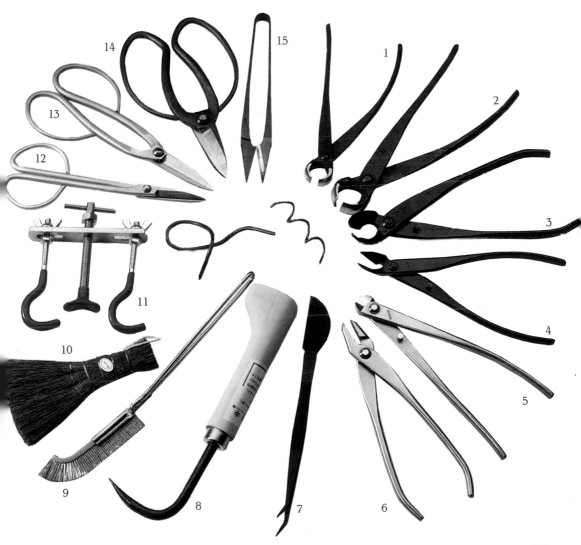

Pruning the branches

The main reason why bonsai plants remain small is because they are regularly pruned. In the wild, similarly, it is possible to find trees that are clearly very old but have remained stunted in growth. When a tree grows alongside an animal track, for example, the animals will regularly chew off the young shoots, so preventing it from growing very high.

Bonsai, unlike their wild equivalents, are not so much chewed back as carefully pruned. And they are pruned in such a way that they develop the growth habit that their creator has in mind.

There are many possible ways of styling a tree. It can have a smooth, spherical crown, or a strangely shaped crown that bears the marks of much weather damage. But whatever shape or style you create, there is one thing all bonsai have in common: they should all look both old and impressive. In a full-sized tree this implies a thick, often heavily gnarled trunk, and branches that open out into a dense crown.

Regular pruning stops the branches becoming thicker; it also improves the structure of the crown. If you want to produce both effects at the same time, this means you have to make some compromises. Young plants should be pruned later in the year than plants which have already developed a good, thick trunk.

The later you prune, the more your tree will grow; and the more it grows, the more water channels it will need to carry nutrients between the roots and the leaves. The trunk grows thicker to accommodate these extra channels. A greater leaf mass also requires larger reserves of energy, which must be stored inside the trunk in the form of starch or other materials. This, again, makes for a thicker trunk.

When pruning thick branches, you will create much larger wounds. As a mature bonsai should not bear any visible signs of such treatment, these wounds should not be so large that they never fully heal. Even on young trees, don't allow shoots to grow so long that any wounds left by pruning will not be able to heal up properly. Think how tall you want your bonsai to grow. If you are planning a large bonsai, it will take longer to grow, and the wound will have more time to heal. If you are planning a small bonsai, it will have less time to heal, and any wounds must be correspondingly smaller.

When creating bonsai, your first priority should be to concentrate on developing a good, thick trunk. At this stage you shouldn't prune too often. However, as soon as the trunk

has reached the right size you should start to prune much more frequently. That way the bonsai will develop a dense crown quite naturally. A really healthy tree should normally grow two or more new branches for each old branch every time it is pruned.

Pruning also encourages new growth. The bud nearest to the wound will invariably sprout a new shoot that will form the tip of the branch — so cut each branch back to just above the bud that's pointing in the direction you want the branch to follow.

The explanation for this lies in a characteristic of trees known as *apical dominance* — a tendency for shoots near the tips of branches to assume a dominant role. Trees produce a hormone at the branch tips that suppresses the development of

Left: *Cover any larger wounds with a Japanese wound sealant, which will peel off as the callus tissue forms over the wound.*

Centre: *After two months the wound will look like this.*

Right: *Here is a similar wound site about two years after the cut was made.*

buds further down the branch. If the end of a branch is removed, then the buds nearest the tip are no longer suppressed by this hormone and take over the dominant role. The more pronounced the apical dominance of a particular species, the fewer buds will sprout near the end of a branch.

For similar reasons, bonsai tend to grow more near the top of the crown than near the bottom. If you don't take various measures to counteract this tendency, the upper branches will soon be thicker than the lower branches. This is the exact opposite of older, more mature trees in the wild, whose lower branches are always the thickest. If your bonsai is to look really natural, then its lower branches must also be thicker than the upper ones — and stay that way.

For this reason the shoots in the upper part of the crown should be cut back further and more often than those lower down. Unfortunately, this in turn will create a larger number of apical shoots, which will tend to suppress the growth of buds lower down. So in the upper third of the tree — preferably in the early spring in the case of outdoor bonsai — the branches should be cut back regularly into the older wood. Even nicely forked branches should be removed so as to keep the branches equally thick throughout the crown.

When you first start to work on a tree from a nursery, you often have to remove many of the branches completely. This is so that you can have all the thicker branches at the bottom, and the thinner ones towards the top. Large wounds heal

particularly quickly if they are made in the early spring when the first leaves begin to sprout (or soon after). Wounds made in the late spring or early summer will also heal quickly on either indoor or outdoor plants.

With conifers you should remove large branches in the winter, because less resin oozes out during that period. However, larches, being deciduous, can be treated in the same way as broadleaves.

All wounds should be properly sealed using a suitable wound sealant (see above). Special bonsai sealants can be obtained from specialist outlets.

 Wounds will normally heal more quickly if they are made in the early spring. So it's usually best to prune the larger branches when spring growth begins — or at least soon after. This is also the best time to tidy up wounds made the previous autumn to ensure that they heal properly.

Pruning the roots

The roots and branches of a tree provide for each other, so they should be kept in the right proportions to one another. This inevitably means that the roots have to be pruned as well as the branches.

Unlike the branches, however, they should be pruned during the dormant winter phase. Most trees respond best to root pruning if it is carried out soon before the first growth begins. You should replace the soil at the same time.

As with the branches in the crown of the tree, the aim of pruning the roots is to produce a dense structure. This means that you can have a large root mass in a small container. Root pruning also serves another important purpose — that of creating a visible root spread at the base of the trunk.

The various stages in the process are shown in the series of pictures above.

First, lift the roots out of the container; the outer roots will be densely matted together, often running in circles around the root ball. Start by carefully disentangling the roots with the help of a root hook (in practice, any small hook will do for this purpose). Some of the old soil will come away in the process.

When all the roots are hanging vertically, you'll find that some of them hang down a long way. Cut these back until all the roots will fit into the container they were intended for, without having to be bent back.

Now cut out the roots that are growing directly below the trunk, so that only the spreading roots are left to feed the plant. In the case of the spreading roots, you should prune back the thicker ones more than the thinner ones; this will produce a more even growth. If you have had to make any large wounds, these should be treated with a suitable wound sealant.

If the crown of the tree is going to grow larger, you can choose a larger container for repotting the plant. Place some netting over the drainage holes so the soil isn't washed out when you water it.

Before repotting the plant, spread a suitable drainage layer of *akadama* or John Innes No 3 across the base of the container. Then place the tree back in the container on a thin layer of a suitable planting compost. With many plants this planting mixture can also include a high proportion of *akadama* or John Innes No 3.

Cutting back the roots of a trident maple and repotting it in a new container — the process is described in more detail below.

At this stage you can make the container more stable by running a length of wire through the drainage holes. This will stop the tree being shaken to and fro by the wind.

Finally, fill up the container with the compost, using a small wooden dibber to push it into the gaps between the roots.

The pruning and repotting process is now complete. However, you can if you wish spread an extra layer of fine soil over the top; this will encourage moss to grow over the surface.

Wiring

Wiring is one of the most effective ways of shaping a bonsai plant to any style you want. By winding a length of wire around a set of branches, you can do more than simply change their shape; you can also ensure that they will retain the shape you have imposed on them. Between two and six months later the branch will be growing too thick for the wire; at this point, before it can cut into the bark, you should remove the wire. Afterwards, in most cases, the branch will retain the shape you wanted.

Many of the Japanese styles can only be achieved with the help of wiring. The exception is the broom style, which can be created from most tree species without any need for wiring; in this case, all you need to do is some careful pruning.

The wire can be made of aluminium, copper or iron. These metals differ mainly in their strength and hardness. Aluminium is the softest of the three, and the least likely to damage the bark, but must be really thick if it's going to hold a branch in position. Bonsai wire is most commonly made of this material. If you ask for bonsai wire at a specialist outlet, you will normally be given aluminium wire that has been anodised; this turns it brown, which means it's not so easily visible when seen from a distance.

Copper wire intended for use with bonsai must first be heated up (annealed) in order to make it pliable. It will then cool and harden as you wind it round the branches. Copper wire is strong enough to use for bending larger branches. Being thinner, however, it can easily cut into the bark — so be sure you've had plenty of practice with wiring before you use it on a valuable tree. In Japan, copper wire is mainly used for wiring conifers. It has recently become available from bonsai dealers in the West, too, but you will always need to specify copper wire when you want it.

Iron wire is much cheaper, but it's also harder and more difficult to work with. It also tends to rust, and to leave stains on the bark. Although often used in China, it is rarely used for bonsai in the West.

Outdoor broadleaves and larches should be wired just as soon as the tiny leaf shoots appear in spring. The other conifers can easily be wired in the winter. Indoor bonsai can be wired at any time of year.

Bending the branches can sometimes rupture the water vessels that run through them. These quickly regenerate, but water transfer may be badly disrupted in the meantime. If you've just wired a plant, it's best to keep it in a sheltered, well-shaded position for two to four weeks; that way its water reserves aren't likely to be overstretched.

You must always be sure to keep a close eye on trees that have been wired. If their branches are growing thicker — as they do on outdoor bonsai in June or in autumn — the wiring will quickly become too tight. It should therefore be removed before it starts biting into the bark tissue.

With indoor bonsai this can happen after as little as two months. If the branch doesn't stay in the position that you want when the wire is removed, then you can always wire it a second time.

From above to far left: *Sycamore branches can be wired up like this.*

Above right: *Tensioned wires should be secured firmly by means of strong wire loops.*

Far right: *Pass tensioned wire through plastic tubing so as to protect the branch.*

Right: *If you don't remove the wire soon enough, the branches will remain visibly scarred.*

Wiring procedure

It's always best to use thick wires for older, thicker branches and thinner wires for younger, thinner ones.

Wind the wires around each branch into a spiral configuration. Wind them in the same direction all over the tree, and never allow any wires to cross. If you need to run two wires along the same branch, then you should wind them parallel to each other. If possible, run each length of wire along two branches.

If a branch is too thick to be corrected by wiring, then you can pull it into the shape that you want by means of thin tensioned wire. This procedure is shown in the pictures at top right, and is also described in more detail on pages 38–39.

You should always use plastic tubing to cushion the wire around the branch so that it doesn't cut into the bark.

Buying bonsai

The use of the term 'bonsai' is not specifically regulated by law. For most people the word has associations with something valuable and expensive, and there are some gardening outlets that take ruthless advantage of this, passing off any tree in a pot as genuine bonsai.

Now it's true that the Japanese words *bon* and *sai*, taken on their own, mean no more than 'tray' and 'plant'. But together they mean much more than just that, summing up the long-cherished tradition of styling trees to imitate nature in miniature — and this is the vital distinguishing feature of bonsai.

This means that anything sold as bonsai should show at least some evidence of such styling. If you want to buy a bonsai plant, there are four main points to consider when you're deciding what to choose:

- the tree species
- the quality of the work carried out on it so far
- the shape
- the price.

The right species

If you don't have a garden or balcony available, you will have to limit yourself to trees that can be kept indoors all year round. If you're a beginner as well, then the best trees to grow indoors are members of the genus *Ficus* — i.e. fig trees. There's a good choice of fig species available as bonsai, all of which are easy to maintain.

If you have a garden, or even just a balcony, then you're best advised to opt for outdoor species. As these are kept in the same or similar climatic conditions to those of their native habitat, they're generally more robust than most indoor bonsai. They also cope better if you make mistakes while you're looking after them, which is inevitable if you're a beginner.

Make sure the light conditions are right for your particular species. If you've chosen a very sunny position, for example, then you should buy a tree that needs lots of sun, such as a pine or an elm.

Quality and shape

Don't buy a tree if there are any major imperfections or signs of poor treatment — if, for example, there is scarring from wires that is visible years after the wires have been removed. If the trunk is thinner at the base than where the first branch forks, this is another fault that will be difficult to put right.

How much should you have to pay?

The price of a bonsai plant will depend on how old it is and how much work has been invested in it. It's difficult for a beginner to guess the age.

However, a bonsai with a thick trunk and large, unhealed wounds is likely to be younger than one which has a trunk that's only half as thick but has no open wounds.

The branching structure is another sign of a tree's age: the finer and denser it is, the older the tree is likely to be. A bonsai tree never reaches a finished state; it is in a continuous process of development. So the more mature it is, the more expensive it will be.

When choosing a tree, you should also consider its development potential. This again depends on how well it's been maintained, and when you buy a tree you assume this responsibility yourself. If you have no idea of its development potential, ask an expert to help you.

If this is your first attempt at bonsai, don't buy a plant that is very old, and therefore expensive. If you ruin it first time round, then a cheaper, younger plant won't be so much of a loss. A younger plant will also be less fixed in its shape, which will give you greater scope for being creative.

If at first you feel out of your depth when it comes to styling the plant, find an expert, or at least a friend with more experience than you, who can help with your first attempts at pruning and wiring.

A Japanese maple may look like this when you buy it from a bonsai specialist.

Propagating from seed

This is by far the most difficult method of creating bonsai, so if you're a beginner you would be well advised to opt for a young nursery plant instead.

If, however, there are no suitable young plants of a particular species available, you may often be forced to grow one from seed. You might, for example, find a particularly good tree while on holiday and decide to create a bonsai from this species, only to discover that young specimens of the plant are simply nowhere to be found. The only solution in this case is to take ripe seeds from the tree itself.

It's some compensation to know that seeds are the easiest parts of a plant to store and transport. Even so, the seeds of different tree species have to be treated in different ways to make them germinate.

Treatment and storage

The first important thing is to protect your seeds from mould. Never keep them in an airtight container. Keep berry fruits well ventilated until you get home, and then dry them when the weather is suitable.

The seeds of some berry fruits won't germinate in the wild until they've passed through the gut of a bird. The best way to reproduce this effect is to crush the berries in water and leave

them to ferment for a few days; then you can sow them out.

Acacia seeds are contained in pods, which should be transported in a bag that allows plenty of air to reach them. Like the scales from the cones of conifers, you should store them in a dry place until it's time to sow them out.

Many seeds, such as acorns, beechmast, walnuts and chestnuts, can't germinate if you dry them out. Store these in a cool place in damp sand until you are able to sow them out.

Other seeds retain their ability to germinate as long as they remain inside their fruits. But as soon as the flesh of the fruit starts to rot, you should remove the seeds. You can store them in cold, damp sand or sow them out straight away.

Sowing

Take a suitable container with drainage holes in the bottom, and fill it up with a sowing medium that is poor in nutrients. You can use either a sowing tray or an ordinary plant pot for sowing purposes.

Press the soil down lightly, place the seeds a suitable distance apart, press them gently into the soil, and finally cover them with another thin layer of soil. Water them generously, and place a clear plastic bag or a cloche over the container.

The soil should be kept evenly moist but not wet, and it should never be allowed to dry out. As soon as the little seedlings appear, you should gradually give them more air, until eventually you can remove the covering completely.

It's important not to let the seedlings become too wet during their first few weeks, or they will quickly die. With sensitive species, you should wait until the soil dries out

before watering again, and then give just enough water to make it slightly moist. It's easier to achieve this by watering from below: place the container in a shallow tray with just a little water in it — that way only the lower layers of the soil will become saturated.

To ensure that the plants are not attacked by fungal infections such as wilt, you can spray a little fungicide over them. Then, about four weeks after germina-tion, you can start applying carefully measured doses of inorganic fertiliser at fortnightly intervals.

Once the seedlings have become strong enough, you can transplant them to individual pots. At this stage it's safe to shorten any vertical roots — this will encourage the development of strong side roots. But don't start pruning the stem or branches until the plant is at least two years old.

From now on your plants can be treated in exactly the same way as bonsai that have been propagated from cuttings (see next page).

Zelkova seedlings, pictured two, four and six years after sowing

Propagating from cuttings

One of the best ways of propagating bonsai is to use cuttings. The idea is to take a small piece of twig and encourage it to take root. The result will be an independent plant with all the same characteristics as the parent plant from which the cutting was taken.

Propagation by grafting and from cuttings are the two most reliable methods if you want to reproduce a pure species or variety of tree.

Some of our native species can be propagated from seed taken from plants growing in the wild.

For instance, you can produce a mountain ash from mountain ash seed. But with a more exotic plant you will often not have access to a male and female partner of the same species, so seeding will not occur. This means the only plant available from seed will be a hybrid of two species.

A similar case arises if you want to propagate a particular variety or cultivar, such as a Japanese maple with a specific leaf pattern.

Trees from cuttings will grow less readily than grafted trees, which is why professional growers prefer grafts. But with bonsai you are more interested in a good-looking trunk than a fast-growing plant. Besides which, grafting often leaves a permanent blemish on the trunk — a problem that's easily avoided with cuttings.

Always use cuttings with the leaves or needles still on them. With indoor plants you can obtain these at any time of year. June is the best time for taking cuttings from outdoor trees, although most conifers provide

Cuttings will root easily if you pot them up like this.

successful cuttings even in the middle of winter.

The best cuttings to use are semi-ripe ones — i.e. those obtained from parts of the current year's growth that have just started to become woody. Moreover, cuttings from tip shoots often root better than those taken from side shoots.

Propagation procedure

Always pot your cuttings in soil that is poor in nutrients. This will encourage them to form longer roots in the search for more nutrients.

The best commercially available medium is cuttings compost. However, you can easily make up a suitable cuttings mixture yourself using a combination of sand and peat — or a peat substitute.

Use a container with suitable drainage holes; a flower pot will do nicely. Press the soil down gently and use a small wooden dibber to create suitable holes for your cuttings.

Take cuttings 2-3 in (5-9 cm) long, and remove the leaves or needles from the lower part of each stem. Dip the cut end of each cutting in a rooting hormone (though this is not always necessary) and place the cutting in a planting hole, pressing the soil in gently around it.

Finally, water the pot carefully and put a clear plastic bag over it. Place the pot in a warm, well-lit position.

If the cuttings start to grow, this usually means they have started to root. Now you can

The cutting on the left has already developed roots.

gradually give them more air. Begin by making small holes in the plastic; later on, you can increase the size of the holes. Once the plants have grown an inch or so (a few centimetres), you can start to give them a carefully measured feed.

Later on, when your cuttings are fully developed and have established roots, you can plant them out individually. Cuttings don't usually form vertical roots; their roots normally spread out evenly in all directions. But you should still prune the longer roots at this stage so that the shorter ones have a chance to catch up, producing a more even spread later on.

Early on in their development, the cuttings can be modified towards the style you envisage for your bonsai. For example, if you want to create an upright-style tree with a nice tapering trunk, you should keep pruning the trunk down to the first

branch. That way the branch will take over the role of the trunk every time.

If you want to create a broom-style tree, you should cut the trunk back to the point where the base of the crown is intended to be. The branches immediately below the wound can be used to form the crown. However, the branches further down can also be left for a while to help the trunk in this section grow thicker. They don't need to be removed until later on — although you should always bear in mind that the longer you wait, the bigger the eventual wounds will be.

Using nursery plants

You can save a lot of time by using a plant that is mature but untrained. This may be a nursery plant, a potted plant from a flower shop or garden centre, or a so-called 'raw plant' from a specialist bonsai outlet.

With outdoor bonsai the best time to look for a suitable candidate is between the first autumn colours of September and the first new shoots in the spring. With indoor bonsai you can start at any time of year.

When choosing a plant, you should take particular note of the existing root spread, the shape of the trunk and the structure of the lower branches. Once you have obtained a suitable plant, you can start styling it straight away.

You first need to choose which side of the plant should be at the front. Your decision in this will be affected by the direction of the root spread, the shape of the trunk and the positions of the branches.

If possible, the strongest roots should be growing to the left and right — not forwards — and the trunk should have an interesting shape. The main branches should be easy to distinguish, and they should each emerge from a different point on the trunk.

Having chosen the front of your plant, you must now decide on a suitable container for it (if you don't already have one). The roots shouldn't be heavily pruned until some time later, so in the meantime the container should be large enough to accommodate the existing roots without too much difficulty — and the tree will also grow much faster in a bigger container.

Now you need to choose which branches to remove. Always follow the principle of keeping the thickest branches lower down and the thinnest near the tip. At every point on the trunk where there is more than one branch, remove the thinner branches towards the bottom of the crown and the thicker ones towards the top. It may also be very helpful to consider the typical characteristics of the particular style that you have in mind.

Once you have removed all the superfluous branches, it's time to think about shaping

those that remain. Most trees react well to wiring if you do this around the time of the first spring growth.

At other times of year, however, it's safer for a beginner to pull the branches into shape using tensioned wire (see also page 31). For this you'll need to find some way of securing the wires. With a wooden container you can use nails. With a plastic container you can make holes where loops of strong, thick wire can be secured. If you have a proper bonsai container, then the drainage holes can serve the same purpose.

The tensioned wire should be as thin as possible. To protect the bark, slide some plastic tubing over the top loop of the wire before you hook it over the branch. Pull the wire down to bring the branch into the correct position, and fix the other end to the container using a loop of thick wire.

Once the branches have been bent into the right shape, you can prune them to the length

Creating a bonsai out of a small juniper spaling obtained from a nursery: this involves both pruning and wiring, and the end result looks extremely convincing.

you require. Keep the plant for a fortnight in a well-lit but shaded position so that it has time to get accustomed to its new shape.

From now on the bonsai can be treated normally, depending on the season. If winter's already approaching, you can plant an outdoor tree in a garden bed or some other outdoor position such as a balcony. If it's spring, and growth has already begun, you can start to apply fertiliser. At this stage you can also wire any of the thinner side branches that have not already been shaped using tensioned wire.

Pruning during the first summer will depend on how the branches are to be incorporated into the crown of the tree. This will normally mean heavier pruning at the top of the crown than towards the base. Any branches that need to grow thicker should be left unpruned until they have reached the thickness you want.

If the tree is sufficiently developed by the following spring, then it will be ready for transplanting to a suitable bonsai container.

Using wild plants (yamadori)

The original method of creating bonsai was to go out and find a wild plant that you could dig up and bring home. Some of the oldest and most valuable bonsai in Japan have been created from such plants.

Old trees that have remained small are by no means rare in the wild. Where game animals have made paths through the forests, these are often lined by small beeches that have been nibbled continually by passing animals. These specimens usually develop a short, thick trunk and a small, densely branching crown.

On mountain slopes, too, you can find ancient trees whose growth has remained stunted. These are normally conifers, and their unusually small stature is normally due to environmental factors such as a shortage of available soil.

One of the most striking features of these ancient trees is the unusual thickness of the bark, which underlines the great age of any bonsai created from them. Often it is the beautiful patterns produced by the bark on a trunk that provide the initial inspiration for using a wild tree from which to create a bonsai plant.

For conservation reasons it is illegal to remove trees from the wild without first obtaining the permission of the landlord. If you find a suitable tree, you will then need a permit from the authority responsible for the land before you can go ahead and dig it up. In many cases the owners will be the Forestry Commission.

The roots of a wild tree are quite unlike the tight root balls possessed by a typical nursery specimen. On the contrary, they are often particularly sparse in the vicinity of the trunk. For this reason you will have to make long and careful preparations before you can go ahead and uproot a wild tree.

In the spring, a whole year before moving the tree, you should cut back about a third of the roots. Use a sharp spade, a saw or a strong branch cutter, and cut them back to about 8–12 in (20–30 cm) from the trunk. When you've finished, cover up the roots again with plenty of soil.

Early the following autumn (around late September), you should cut back another third of the roots. The purpose of this is to encourage the tree to grow extra side roots, which will help it to cope with being uprooted early the following spring. The best time for lifting most trees is just before the first buds begin to swell — i.e. well before the leaves actually sprout.

Once a tree has been dug up, all the branches of a larch or a foliage tree should be pruned well back. Branches that aren't needed for styling can be removed completely.

The next stage is to plant the tree in the garden for a year. If you don't have a garden, then a large trough will do.

During the first few years after transplanting, the tree will need to develop strong roots. It should be fed sparingly at first, and later much more generously. At the same time you should cut back the branches to produce a more compact crown. Plenty of branches next to the trunk will give you more scope for later styling.

When the tree starts to develop healthy growth, this shows the roots have fully regenerated and that it has survived the traumas of transplantation. Now is the time to begin styling the tree, and from this point on you can proceed exactly as you would with a nursery tree.

Move the tree to a smaller container in the early spring, as soon as you have chosen which side is to be at the front. A bonsai container may well be appropriate at this stage. Remove all the superfluous branches, and start to shape the remaining ones, either by wiring them or by pulling them down with tensioned wire. Finally, prune them back to the length that you want.

For the first two weeks at least, you should keep the tree in a sheltered but well-lit position. Only then should you move it to a sunny or semi-shaded position, depending on what its natural requirements are. Now is the time to start giving it regular feeds.

For the next two years you should continue to prune the tree regularly, wiring branches where necessary to achieve the correct shape — and creating jins (see page 24) where you feel they are appropriate.

Then, provided the tree has achieved a certain degree of maturity, you can finally move it to the bonsai container that is just right for it.

A common juniper (Juniperus communis)

If you want to create a bonsai from a wild plant, you'll need to make careful preparations beforehand. To start with, you will need permission from the owner of the land where the plant is growing. Then you will need the right tools to dig up the plant in the correct way and at the right time of year, which is usually spring.

Field maple

The field maple (*Acer campestre*), one of our many native trees, is often used as a hedge plant. A mature solitary has a short trunk bearing a spherical crown.

The flowers are insignificant, and appear in May. The leaves are relatively small (1-2 in; 3-5 cm) and symmetrically arranged; each is made up of three to five lobes. They sprout in May, shortly before the flowers (or at the same time), and turn bright yellow or orange in the autumn. The branches are often ridged with cork. On older trunks the bark becomes rough and very heavily patterned.

Bonsai requirements
The field maple likes sun or semi-shade, and is well suited to exposed positions.

As long as it isn't kept under cover and gets plenty of rain, it can be watered with hard water from the tap. It tolerates soil with high salt concentrations, so it can usually withstand summer drought without the leaves being damaged.

The most suitable soil mixture is a 2:1:1 combination of *akadama* or John Innes No 3, sand and planting compost. Up to about two-thirds of the soil should be replaced at least every other year.

Feed this tree from May to August with organic bonsai fertiliser. At the end of August,

change to a low-nitrogen, high-potassium feed in order to harden it up for the autumn.

Overwinter the tree out of doors, planting it outside its container in a shady spot in the garden, or in a trough filled with sand and peat substitute.

Styles
Among the Japanese styles, the broom style is much the closest to the tree's natural growth habit. However, the upright style is also quite possible, and several other styles may be equally suitable.

Wiring
As with all *Acer* species, the bark of the field maple is very sensitive, so careful wiring is essential — if the wires are too tight, they will often leave the bark permanently scarred.

To avoid this happening, keep a continual eye on the wires. Normally only the one-year-old branches are still flexible enough to be wired. Older branches should be pulled into shape using tensioned wire.

Pruning
Prune all the branches as heavily as you can early in the spring, before growth begins, always bearing in mind how much growth you anticipate for the coming year.

This pruning should be such that it gives the remaining buds

ample space so that new growth isn't obscured by other shoots.

The timing of further pruning depends on the tree's state of development. If the trunk needs to be thicker, then wait until each shoot is some 8 in (20 cm) long and cut back to about two or three leaf pairs. If you're aiming for finer branching, cut back as soon as the shoots reach 4 in (10 cm).

The shoots normally regrow some 2-3 weeks after pruning, so you should prune them for the last time at the end of July. Pinch out any later growth, and this will normally prevent any further growth after that.

Field maples are best able to tolerate leaf cutting in May. Don't remove thicker branches before the spring growth, or the sap may run too much.

Obtaining plants
Collect the seed from August onwards, store it in damp sand in a refrigerator and sow it out in spring.

Older bonsai specimens, often beautifully formed, can be obtained from specialist bonsai outlets.

This eight-year-old field maple has been planted over a rock.

Japanese maple

In its oriental home, the Japanese maple (*Acer palmatum*) is a small tree that grows along the edges of woodlands and on sunny, exposed slopes. The leaves each have five lance-shaped lobes, and sprout very early. They are reddish at first, but soon turn green. They finally turn bright orange to red during the autumn. The trunk is long and smooth, with rough bark that becomes thin and peeling with age.

In Japan this tree has been used for centuries, both for gardens and bonsai displays. Many varieties have been bred for their lovely colouring or interesting shapes.

A. p. 'Deshojo', for example, has bright-red spring foliage, while that of *A. p.* 'Seigen' turns a lovely pink provided it is kept in a well-lit position. The commonest nursery variety is *A. p.* 'Atropurpureum', which sprouts green spring foliage that quickly turns purple in the sun.

Bonsai requirements

As a bonsai the Japanese maple requires a semi-shaded or shaded position sheltered from strong winds. Water it with soft water that is low in salts (e.g. rain water). The leaves develop brown spots if it is watered too much or too little, or if the soil contains too many salts, or if it's exposed to strong winds.

The best soil mixture is a 2:1:1 combination of *akadama* or John Innes No 3, sand and planting compost. Young plants should be given new soil every one to two years. Older trees can be transplanted at rather longer intervals.

Japanese maples are normally winter-hardy, although the roots can be damaged if there are prolonged severe frosts. You should overwinter the plant out of doors and outside its container, placing it in a shady garden bed, or failing that in a trough filled with sand and peat substitute. If the temperature drops below 23°F (-5°C) for any length of time, it's a good idea to cover the tree with an extra layer of protective straw or plastic sheeting.

Styles

Most Japanese styles are possible. Among the most frequently used are informal upright, twin trunks and multiple trunks.

Wiring

One-year-old branches can be wired. However, the bark is very sensitive and easily damaged by the wire, resulting in permanent scarring. The marks left by pressure points, or where the wire bites into the trunk, remain visible for a very long time. The branch thickens especially quickly towards the top of the crown, which can make the wires too tight as early as May. For this reason, older branches should preferably be pulled into shape by means of tensioned wire.

Pruning

As with the field maple, you should remove larger branches when the spring growth begins. If you do this any earlier, the sap will run too much, and the wounds will not heal nearly so well or so quickly.

The branches of young, developing plants should be pruned when they reach a length of 8-10 in (20-25 cm). How much

 If you have a healthy Japanese maple with a thick enough trunk, then the branches will normally benefit from a little leaf cutting. You should do this by May at the latest.

you cut back will depend very much on how much the branch has developed and what part of the crown it is eventually intended to occupy.

More mature plants can be pinched out as soon as growth begins. Remove the shoot tip with tweezers as soon as the second or third leaf pair has started to develop — this produces denser foliage and finer branching. Leaf cutting can also be employed in order to produce smaller leaves on secondary growth.

Obtaining plants

When growing this plant from seed, note that it often doesn't germinate until the second year.

Young plants are readily available from bonsai specialists. Suitable young plants can often be obtained from nurseries, too. Bonsai specialists offer older, styled bonsai at various stages of development and at corresponding prices.

A 20-year-old Japanese maple — height 2 ft (60 cm)

Trident maple

The trident maple (*Acer buergerianum*) is an oriental species that often lines the streets of Japanese cities. The leaves each have three lobes with smooth edges. They are reddish in the spring, turning green in the summer, and orange to purple in the autumn.

The trunk becomes very thick with age, and the bark peels, rather like that of a plane tree, exposing orange areas underneath. The trident maple is sometimes grown in parks.

Bonsai requirements

In Japan, the trident maple is one of the most commonly used broadleaves for traditional bonsai. It is ideal in that its leaves tend to be unusually small, and even large wounds will heal extremely quickly. This has made it equally popular for bonsai in the West.

Out of doors, the trident maple needs an open, sunny position that is shaded only around midday. It needs plenty of wind and breezes to make the leaves stronger and more resistant to diseases.

You should use a suitably porous planting medium such as a 3:1:1 combination of *akadama* or John Innes No 3, sand and planting compost. However, other combinations have also proved successful.

The unusually strong root growth means that this tree uses up large amounts of water. Give it water that is low in salts, such as rain water or soft tap water.

You should also provide it with plenty of fertiliser in the form of a solid organic bonsai feed. (Osmacote has proved very good for this purpose.)

Overwinter the tree outside its container, planting it in the garden or on a balcony in a trough filled with a mixture of sand and peat substitute.

If the temperature drops below 23°F (-5°C) on the balcony — or below 14°F (-10°C) in the garden bed — then you should cover the tree with an extra protective layer of leaves, twigs, straw or plastic sheeting.

Styles

If you buy a trident maple, it will usually have been styled already. The upright style is the norm, although twin trunks and multiple trunks are also regularly available. Other styles and growth habits are similarly possible.

Wiring

It is still possible to wire one- or two-year-old branches. However, older, more rigid branches should be pulled into shape using tensioned wire.

The branches thicken very quickly, so you should also check them regularly to make sure the wire hasn't started cutting into the bark.

Pruning

If large branches have to be removed in the early stages of shaping the tree, you should do this during or soon after the first spring growth. The wounds will heal much faster at this stage, provided you use a good wound sealant.

Young, developing plants should generally be pruned when the spring shoots are at least 4-6 in (10-15 cm) long. The new growth will appear about two weeks after this, and should be treated similarly.

More mature trees can be pruned when the shoots are only 2 in (5 cm) long, or can be pinched out when the second leaf pair appears. From August onwards, pinch out any further growth that occurs.

Leaf cutting to encourage finer branching is a task best under-taken in May.

Obtaining plants

The seed is difficult to get hold of. However, the trident maple can easily be propagated from cuttings. Use semi-ripe shoot tips for this purpose.

Young plants are readily available from bonsai specialists, but nurseries will rarely have them. Older, pre-styled imported trees are generally on offer at specialist outlets.

A 15-year-old trident maple planted on a rock

Birch

Under normal conditions most birches (*Betula*) grow into slender, graceful trees with trunks covered in white bark. The silver birch (*B. pendula*) also develops upward-growing branches with drooping shoots. Birches can grow to 60 ft (20 m) or more. When the leaves drop the warted branches make them very easy to recognise.

The leaves often don't appear until shortly after flowering in April or May. Their autumn colouring varies from bright yellow to orange. Birches are monoecious (i.e. with separate male and female flowers on the same tree) and rely on the wind for pollination. The fruits are winged nuts that ripen in June and are dispersed by the wind.

The birch is one of the few trees that most people can name on sight; for this reason it's also very popular for bonsai. Of our native birches, only two will naturally develop the white trunk and characteristic growth habit: the silver birch and the downy birch (*B. pubescens*). The dwarf birch (*B. nana*), with its shrubbier habit, bears small, roundish leaves. Many imported species with white trunks can be found in gardens and parks — too many to name them all here. Besides, there is a great deal of spontaneous hybridisation, so it's often very difficult to determine the exact provenance of a particular specimen.

Bonsai requirements
Birches need a sunny but airy position that doesn't trap the heat on hot days. The soil can be of almost any kind, but there must be good drainage to allow excess water to escape. Birches can't cope with frost if the roots have just been pruned, so transplant them when spring growth has just begun.

Birches consume a great deal of water. You *can* use tap water, but the plant is sensitive to salts, and will then need a lot of excess water to flush them out — so all in all you may be better off using rain water. If the roots dry out, or the plant becomes too hot, it reacts by dropping

the inside leaves. Feed it fortnightly from the first spring growth through to the beginning of August.

Once a birch has shed its leaves, it is extremely frost-hardy. However, in very cold

areas you may have to remove it from its container as soon as the leaves have dropped, and bury the roots in a garden bed or a large trough.

Styles

If any wound is not carefully sealed, it is likely to provide a pathway for infections for a considerable time after pruning — and if this happens the branch will die. But as long as you bear this point in mind, a birch is easy to shape.

Any style is possible. A silver birch looks most natural with a slender crown and branches that droop at the ends, but in most birch bonsai, including older specimens, the branches tend to grow upwards instead of drooping. This means you may have to wire all new growth, as on a bonsai it won't be heavy enough to droop naturally.

Wiring

Young branches can easily be wired. With older branches, however, it's better to pull them into shape using tensioned wire. So if you want to wire older

A 10-year-old dwarf birch growing over a rock

branches, it's best to do this during the first spring growth. This is the period when any breaches in the plant's internal water channels will heal most quickly and effectively.

Pruning

A well-fed birch will regenerate within four weeks of pruning. Thicker branches are best removed during the main growth period, i.e. between April and June. From August onwards, pinch out new shoots to stop any further growth. If the frosts begin before the leaves change colour in the autumn, then the plant will need protection at temperatures below 28°F (-2°C).

Obtaining plants

Ripe seed can be overwintered in dry conditions and sown out in the spring. In the summer, small birch seedlings can normally be found on the surface soil of any window box or bonsai container. Young birch plants are regularly available from most bonsai specialists.

If you want a silver birch (*B. pendula*) or a downy birch (*B. pubescens*) to develop white bark, then you should start the tree off in the garden, where you can begin to shape it straight away. Don't transfer it to a container until the bark is white.

Hornbeam

The common or European hornbeam (*Carpinus betulus*) is a small tree about 15–30 ft (5–10 m) high, though it occasionally grows to 80 ft (25 m). It often develops multiple trunks, and (if it's grown in the open) an oval-shaped crown. The trunk is often twisted and gnarled, and the bark tends to become silvery with age, peeling off vertically to create an interesting pattern of stripes.

The female flowers are pollinated on the wind. They develop nut-like seeds, each connected to a three-lobed 'wing' so that they, too, can be dispersed on the wind. The oval-shaped leaves, arranged alternately, have a doubly serrated edge, and appear in late April or early May. In the autumn they turn bright yellow and later brown, but remain on the tree throughout the winter until the new shoots appear in the spring.

The leaves and fruits of the hornbeam

Bonsai requirements

Closely related to the birch, the hornbeam is mainly used as a hedge plant. It is among the most popular European bonsai species, mainly because of its strong growth potential and its tolerance of pruning.

The hornbeam likes an airy, semi-shaded position in the open air all year round. It is not fussy about soil. A mixture of equal portions by weight of *akadama* or John Innes No 3,

sand and planting compost is commonly used. For young plants, replace two-thirds of the soil at least every other year. Older, more mature plants can be transplanted at longer intervals. The soil often contains a fungus that produces mushroom-like fruiting bodies in the late summer. This fungus forms a symbiotic (mutually beneficial) relationship with the tree.

It's best to water a hornbeam with rain water, but you can use tap water as long as the plant gets plenty of rain directly. If there's a long dry period, you should avoid using hard water or water that is high in salts, as this will cause the leaves to turn brown around the edges.

Hornbeams need a lot of feeding. Organic fertiliser in powdered or granulated form has often proved very successful. Feed generously from the appearance of the first leaf shoots through to the end of June. If the plant still shows

signs of deficiencies, add a carefully measured amount of inorganic fertiliser (but take care, as the hornbeam is sensitive to salts).

Overwinter the tree outside its container, either in the garden or in a trough filled with sand and peat substitute. If the temperature drops below 14°F (–10°C), then you should cover the plant with plastic sheeting, straw or fir twigs.

Styles

All Japanese styles are suitable for the hornbeam, but the commonest is the upright form. This can be obtained from a young plant without wiring — i.e. by means of carefully organised pruning.

Wiring

This is usually necessary only for older plants. One- or two-year-old branches can usually

be bent successfully, although •
the wire can easily cut into the
bark. Older branches can only
be pulled into shape.

Pruning

Remove thick branches in the
spring, preferably just before the
first shoots appear; that way the
wounds will heal much more
quickly. You can prune the new
growth when it's between 2 in
(5 cm) and 12 in (30 cm) long,
depending on the style you're
aiming for. The longer you let it
grow, the thicker the branches
become. The hornbeam regrows
quickly every time you cut, so
you can achieve a dense crown
in a relatively short time.

Provided you feed the soil
enough, you can cut the leaves
as little as four weeks after the
first spring growth — although
this will stop the branches
growing any thicker.

Obtaining plants

Collect the seed in the autumn,
overwinter it in damp sand in
the refrigerator, and sow out in
the spring.

Both young plants and older,
styled specimens can be obtained from specialist outlets.

*This 25-year-old hornbeam is about
30 in (80 cm) tall.*

Cotoneaster

Cotoneasters (*Cotoneaster*) are medium-sized ornamental shrubs with small leaves. They develop a variety of growth habits, and can often be found in gardens and parks. Their native habitats cover much of Europe, North Africa and Asia, and they include both deciduous and evergreen species.

The flower colour varies between white and red, while the fruit ranges from red through orange to yellow.

Bonsai requirements

Cotoneasters should be kept outdoors throughout the year. They prefer a sunny or semi-shaded position, and are also tolerant of wind.

When it comes to soil, cotoneasters aren't particularly demanding. They grow well, for example, in pure *akadama* or John Innes No 3, or in a combination of equal portions of *akadama* (or No 3), sand and planting compost. Other well-drained mixtures can also be used — it's important to avoid waterlogging.

The best time to water cotoneasters is when the soil is slightly dry, as they can cope with short periods of dryness. They are tolerant of hard tap water, and will even benefit from soil containing lime. Feed them from April until August with either an organic or an inorganic fertiliser.

Overwinter the plants in the open air outside their containers, either in the garden or in a trough on the balcony. If the temperature drops below 14°F (-10°C), then evergreen species should be protected with leaves, straw or plastic sheeting.

Styles

Cotoneasters are easy to style. In the wild most (though not all) of them adopt a creeping or shrub-like habit, but they can easily be shaped to whatever style you like.

Because their leaves, flowers and fruits are usually small, cotoneasters make excellent candidates for *mame* pots (special small containers). These trees can also be very good for rock plantings.

Wiring

Branches up to three years old can readily be shaped by means of wiring. Older branches will need to be pulled into shape using tensioned wire.

Pruning

You can prune young, undeveloped plants when the new shoots are 4–6 in (10–15 cm) long. Since they're often forming into side branches by this stage, it may be better to cut back the trunk so that a side branch takes over as the trunk.

Older plants that have already been shaped should be pruned

when the shoots are 2 in (5 cm) long. Cut them back to about fi-1 in (1-2 cm).

If you need to remove older branches during the first stages of styling, then it's best to do this during the early spring growth. This is because the wounds on cotoneasters heal rather slowly, and carrying this out in spring will keep the healing time to a minimum.

Obtaining plants

Remove the seeds from the fruit, overwinter them in damp sand in the refrigerator, and sow them out in the spring. Cotoneasters can easily be propagated from cuttings.

Most garden centres sell a variety of cotoneaster species at different stages of growth. Wild specimens are also easy to find, perhaps even on garden rubbish dumps. Fully styled plants are normally available from bonsai specialists.

This 15-year-old cotoneaster is covered with fruit.

Hawthorn

Hawthorn and may are the common names for a group of shrubs and small trees belonging to the genus *Crataegus*. They include many species, both native and imported, that can be found growing wild in all parts of Europe.

Some hawthorns have irregular trunks like the muscled arms of a high-performance athlete; the complex pattern of ridges reflects the structure of their internal vessels. The bark is dark brown, and tends to peel off in large, flat pieces. The branches are usually very thorny, carrying both surface prickles and actual thorns.

The leaves, arranged alternately, are dark green in colour, turning yellow, orange or red in the winter depending on the species. Some well-known species produce red flowers, others white. After pollination by insects, these develop into attractive red fruits. The number of seeds in each fruit varies depending on how many pistils the original flower contained.

Bonsai requirements

Hawthorns should be kept outdoors all year round. They like a sunny or semi-shaded position, and are very tolerant of wind. They can be kept moderately wet all the time, but are sensitive to salts. This means that if you use tap water, you should give them generous quantities so the excess salts can be flushed out and don't build up in the soil.

The soil mixture can vary. A mixture of equal portions of *akadama* or John Innes No 3, sand and planting compost has produced good results. But the soil has to be porous, so it should not be too fine-grained.

The hawthorn needs high levels of nutrients. Feed it every two weeks from April to July with an organic bonsai fertiliser. In August, change to a low-nitrogen feed — perhaps even a cactus fertiliser.

Overwinter the tree outside its container, either in the garden or in a large trough filled with sand and peat substitute.

The hawthorn or may bears attractive red fruit.

Styles

A hawthorn can be shaped to any style you like, whether Japanese or otherwise, just as long as you start while the plant is still young.

Wiring

Branches up to 0.2 in (5 mm) thick can easily be shaped by wiring. Start wiring when the first spring shoots begin to appear. This also has the advantage that there are no leaves to get in the way.

In most species the branches grow thicker only very slowly, so you can leave the wire on throughout the growing season. If the wire is still not too tight even in the autumn, then you can leave it on throughout the winter. You should then remove it when the first spring shoots appear, and if necessary replace it with new wire.

Pruning

Thicker branches should be removed in the early spring so that they can heal as quickly as possible. Even then, some of the slow-growing species will often take several years to heal properly. Any wounds made on the trunk should be treated with a wound sealant immediately after pruning.

Not all the buds on the branches will grow to form long shoots. Indeed, most of them will stop growing after the first leaves have appeared. Any that do grow longer should be pruned when they reach about 6 in (15 cm). You should cut back to between two and five leaves, depending on the eventual length that you envisage for the branch.

Older plants should be pruned when the shoots are still very short to improve branching.

Obtaining plants

Collect seed from native species in September; remove the flesh of the fruit, and overwinter the seed in damp sand in the refrigerator; sow out in spring. Hawthorn seedlings are often found in gardens, especially near where birds like to perch, e.g. alongside a fence.

Bonsai specialists sell the red-flowered species at various stages of development.

A 25-year-old hawthorn

Beech

The common or European beech (*Fagus sylvatica*) is one of our most important native trees; the Japanese white beech (*F. crenata*) is very closely related. If they are grown as solitaries, both species mature into tall, stately trees with a handsome spherical crown and branches that reach down almost to the ground. The bark is grey in the European beech, silvery in the Japanese species, and remains smooth even on the oldest trees.

The tiny flowers are pollinated on the wind. In the autumn they form triangular nuts, which on the common beech are edible and are known as beechmast.

The wavy-edged leaves are arranged alternately; on the Japanese species they are smaller and narrower. They sprout from an unusually elongated, cinnamon-coloured bud, often appearing as late as the beginning of May. At first they have a velvety covering, but later they lose this almost completely. They turn yellow or orangy-yellow in the autumn, and later brown. Sometimes the foliage stays on the tree throughout the winter, dropping only shortly before the new growth begins.

Bonsai requirements

Both species prefer a semi-shaded position that is protected from the midday sun. They also need shelter from strong winds. Beeches are very sensitive to salts, so you should water them with rain water or any other water that is low in salts. If you only have tap water available, give the tree generous amounts so that any excess salts are flushed out and don't accumulate in the soil.

Apply plenty of fertiliser from the moment the spring shoots appear. Choose a feed that is fairly high in potassium, as this will help protect the leaves from excess transpiration. A good soil combination is a mixture of equal proportions of *akadama* or John Innes No 3, sand and

This European beech is some 25 years old.

planting compost. You should transplant your beeches at least every other year.

Overwinter the plants outside their containers, either in a shady bed in the garden or in a trough on the balcony filled with sand and peat substitute. If there are prolonged cold spells with temperatures below 14°F (-10°C), then you should cover the plants with an extra layer of straw, twigs or plastic sheeting.

Styles
The upright style is much the closest to the natural growth habit of the beech. However, most other Japanese styles are equally possible.

Pruning
As soon as the first shoots are fully developed, cut them back, usually to about one or two leaves (except where you want a longer branch). The shoots will re-form within three weeks of the first pruning, and you should cut them back again to about one or two leaves.

The leaves remaining on the tree tend to grow very large, so as long as the plant is healthy and well fed, you should cut the leaves after a gap of another two weeks. Do remember, though, that without leaves the tree can't cope with direct sunlight. Keep it fully shaded until the new shoots appear. As the top branches grow faster than those lower down, you should always prune the higher branches earlier than those near the base of the crown.

It's best to cut thicker branches in the spring, shortly before growth begins; treat the wounds with a good wound sealant to speed up the healing process.

Wiring
You need to be very careful when wiring a beech. The bark is easily damaged, and tight wires often leave permanent scars. The branches grow suddenly thicker in June, and the wires may cut the bark if you take your eyes off them for only a few days. If possible, avoid wiring altogether, and just use tensioned wire to pull the branches into shape.

This 15-year-old Japanese white beech looks attractive even without its leaves.

Obtaining plants
You can collect the beech mast in the autumn, overwinter the seeds in damp sand in the refrigerator, and sow out in the spring. However, you shouldn't start pruning the new plant for at least two years.

Bonsai specialists offer a wide choice of specimens of both the common beech and the Japanese white beech.

Crab apple

The crab apple (*Malus* species and varieties) is one of our oldest cultivated trees. Older specimens develop a broad, characteristically flat-topped crown that is often very irregular in shape. The bark is heavily ridged, and tends to break off as the plant becomes older and more mature.

The flowers are pinkish at first, later becoming white; they grow on special short shoots soon after the leaves have appeared in May. After pollination by insects, they develop into those familiar fruits. The apples vary greatly in colour, size and number, depending on the species or variety.

The leaves are generally elliptical, with serrated edges and slightly downy undersides. There are many varieties with red-coloured leaves. The autumn colouring varies from a pale orange to a dirty-looking yellowish brown.

Bonsai requirements

It is normal to use small-fruited varieties for bonsai. They need a sunny, airy position.

The crab apple requires a tremendous amount of water, and is invariably the first tree to develop that tell-tale droop in hot weather — a sure sign of water deficiency. However, it is also a lime-loving tree, which means you can always water it with hard water.

A bonsai from a crab apple often bears a lot of fruit.

For soil you can use a standard bonsai mixture made up of equal portions of *akadama* or John Innes No 3, sand and planting compost. As the tree needs so much water, you should not choose too small a container; the soil must be able to store enough water for the plant's daily needs.

Feed the plant with a solid organic bonsai fertiliser (granules, for example) from May through to the middle of August. If you're careful, you can also use an inorganic feed. And provided the plant is well fed, it will continue to sprout after every pruning right through into late summer.

Overwinter your apple tree outside its container, either in a shady spot in the garden, or in a large trough on the balcony filled with sand and some form of peat substitute.

Styles

Apple-tree bonsai imported from Japan are characterised by a short, thick trunk with thick, mainly unforked branches covered with blossom (and later with fruit). This means that they aren't in the least like any apple tree that has grown naturally in the West. However, the crab apple can be shaped just like other trees. The best forms are the ordinary broom style and the upright style.

Pruning

Depending on the age of the tree, the shoots should be pruned when they reach a length of between 2 in (5 cm) and 4 in (10 cm). You should keep at least one leaf on each shoot to prevent the short shoots from flowering until the following year.

After drastic summer pruning, you will occasionally find that a shoot intended to flower the following spring will come into blossom. This results in the tree bearing ripe fruits and blossom at one and the same time.

Older branches should be cut back in the early spring, since this is the time when wounds will heal most quickly.

Wiring

Only one- or two-year-old branches can be bent to the desired shape by means of wiring. Thicker branches unfortunately tend to be damaged by this procedure, so it's best to pull them into shape using tensioned wire.

Obtaining plants

Collect the seeds from the apple cores in the autumn, and over-winter them in damp sand in the refrigerator; sow out in the spring. Bear in mind that most apple trees are grafted, which means you won't get the same tree variety as the one from which the seed has been taken.

You are more likely to get the tree variety you want if you buy a young plant from a specialist bonsai outlet, where you'll find plenty of varieties at different stages of development.

An 18-year-old crab apple — always use a small-fruited variety so that the fruits are more in proportion with the size of the tree.

Oak

Most oaks (*Quercus* species) can survive to a great age. If they're grown as solitaries, they will develop a short, thick trunk covered in rough bark, and a broad, spreading crown. The branches are gnarled and mis-shapen, but relatively open in structure. The leaves have irregular lobes, and those on Mediterranean species have a spike at the tip.

A tree produces separate male and female flowers in the early spring. The male flowers consist of greenish-yellow catkins, each hanging near a single female flower. After successful wind pollination, the female flowers develop into acorns. On the English oak (*Q. robur*) the acorns hang on long stalks in small groups, while on the sessile oak (*Q. petraea*) they form large, grape-like clusters.

Bonsai requirements

Oaks are so much a part of our culture that no British bonsai collection should be without one. However, there are so many species that there is only room here to consider the two commonest ones: the sessile or durmast oak and the common or English oak.

These two species should be kept in the open air all year round. They prefer a sunny or semi-shaded location without too much shelter, and will thrive in even the windiest position.

They are salt-tolerant and lime-loving, so you can always water them with tap water. Feed them generously from April through to August, using a solid organic feed such as Osmacote.

The soils can vary; the English oak likes a sandy mixture as much as a loamy one. A combi-nation of equal portions of *akadama* or John Innes No 3, sand and planting compost has proved very effective. Young plants should be given new soil every other year so that they develop as quickly as possible. The best time for repotting is between February and April; oaks should never be trans-planted in the autumn.

When grown as bonsai, oaks have proved surprisingly frost-sensitive, so the roots, at least, should be well protected. It's best to overwinter weakened plants in a frost-free position — although at the same time you should avoid the risk of fungal infections by removing all the leaves and spraying the tree with a suitable fungicide.

This 25-year-old oak has been grown as a semi-cascade-style bonsai.

Styles

Oaks can be shaped to any suitable style or growth habit.

Wiring

One-year-old branches are suitable candidates for wiring, but they quickly grow thicker; check the wiring regularly and prevent it from cutting into the bark, as this might leave visible scarring. Older branches should be pulled into shape with tensioned wire.

Pruning

Oaks tolerate pruning very well. However, the shoots towards the top of the crown always dominate, so branches that have grown during the preceding year should be reduced to the same length as those lower down. You should also remove the end bud of any branch that you want to fork.

If the trunk hasn't yet reached the thickness that you want, then the spring shoots should be allowed to grow to at least 8–12 in (20–30 cm). However, the first pruning can be carried out within three weeks of the first spring growth. If the tree is properly fed, then the shoots should grow again within three weeks of any pruning.

Obtaining plants

Collect the acorns in September and/or October, overwinter them in damp sand in the refrigerator, and sow them out in the early spring.

Bonsai specialists sell unstyled English oaks of various ages. These usually constitute the best bonsai material.

Small-leaved lime

Under natural conditions the small-leaved lime (*Tilia cordata*) grows to a height of 30–100 ft (10–30 m), with several main branches growing upwards. Each of these produces a series of horizontal side branches. If grown as a solitary, the tree forms a broad, spreading crown.

The heart-shaped leaves are relatively small and arranged alternately. They appear in May, eventually turning bright yellow in the autumn.

The yellowish-white flowers are hermaphrodite. Although popular with bees, they don't appear until the end of June or early July. Each of the pea-sized fruits has a leaflet attached, which enables the seed to be dispersed on the wind.

Bonsai requirements
The small-leaved lime lives up to its name, and for this reason it is the most suitable (and indeed the most popular) *Tilia* species for bonsai.

Although it likes a sunny position in the wild, it is sensitive to salts, so as a bonsai it will need a semi-shaded position in the open air. If you have rain water available, this is particularly beneficial to leaf formation, as the foliage takes up hardly any salts. Limes like plenty of water, but you should avoid waterlogging.

The best soil mixture can be obtained by combining one portion of planting compost with two of *akadama* or John Innes No 3, and just a little sand — although other combinations will also work. Young plants should be repotted at least once every other year.

Adequate feeding is essential for the tree to develop properly. The fertiliser should be predominantly organic in nature. However, carefully measured amounts of inorganic fertiliser should be added to this during the first spring growth, or where poor weather conditions mean that the nutrients from organic feeds are not available quickly enough. From August to mid-September, use a low-nitrogen, high-potassium feed to prepare the tree for winter.

Overwinter the plant outside its container, either in a shaded bed in the garden, or in a trough on the balcony filled with sand and a peat substitute. If the temperature drops below 14°F (-10°C), then you should cover the tree with an additional protective layer of leaves, twigs or plastic sheeting.

Styles
In theory, all styles are possible. Of the traditional Japanese styles, the broom style is closest to the tree's natural growth habit. However, various other forms such as the upright syle and twin trunks are also extremely popular.

Pruning
The small-leaved lime is extremely tolerant of pruning. Shoots regrow within three weeks of each pruning. With sufficient feeding, a young tree without many branches should be able to regrow between three and five times in a year. You should stop pruning by the end of August at the latest — or at least pinch out any further growth. This is so that the shoots have time to harden up for the winter.

Larger branches should be removed either in the spring or during the main growth period, because they will heal most effectively at this stage of the year. However, any larger wounds must always be treated with a good sealant.

In May or June, a healthy tree will react well to leaf cutting, which will improve branching and reduce leaf size. However, this does tend to stop the trunk growing thicker, so you should avoid cutting the leaves until the trunk has achieved the girth that you require.

Wiring
If wiring is needed to shape the branches, then the best time to do it is during the main growth period. You need to be very careful, however, as the bark is extremely sensitive and any

This small-leaved lime is about 15 years old.

resulting scarring can remain visible for a long time.

Even older branches can be successfully wired. However, branches that are especially thick should be pulled into shape with tensioned wire.

Obtaining plants

The seeds can be collected at the end of September or at the beginning of October. You can store them through the winter, keeping them in damp sand in the refrigerator, and sow them out in the spring. However, you will find that sometimes they won't germinate until the second year.

Usable trees between two and five years old can be obtained from bonsai specialists.

Elm and zelkova

Elms (*Ulmus*) and zelkovas (*Zelkova*) are very closely related to each other (*Z. serrata* is commonly known as the Japanese elm), and as bonsai they require much the same treatment. When grown in the open, these trees generally develop a dense, spreading crown on a rather short, thick trunk that may be either smooth or rough, depending on the individual species.

The flowers are only insignificant, and on our native elms they appear before the leaves. They grow in little bundles, developing after pollination into tiny winged nuts. These in turn are dispersed on the wind, and germinate before the summer is actually finished.

The alternately arranged leaves are oval or ovate, and sometimes asymmetric in form; they appear between April and May. The autumn colouring varies a great deal depending on the species, with shades ranging from bright yellow through orange to dark red.

Bonsai requirements

Elms and zelkovas should always be grown out of doors, but they aren't particularly fussy about siting, and will thrive equally well in full sun or semi-shade. They are similarly tolerant of wind.

Perhaps the best soil is a combination of equal portions of *akadama* or John Innes No 3, sand and planting compost — but they also do well with other mixtures. You should change the soil every other year, whatever the age of the tree.

Elms and zelkovas are generally not oversensitive to salts, so they can be watered with ordinary tap water. They can be kept relatively moist, although (as with most trees) you should avoid waterlogging. If they're in a sunny or windy position, they will naturally need a lot more water. Elms and zelkovas also need lots of nutrients, which means that regular feeding is particularly important.

Overwinter the plant outside its container, either in the garden or in a trough filled with sand and peat substitute. If temperatures drop below 23°F (-5°C), cover the tree with a protective layer of leaves, fir twigs or plastic sheeting.

Pruning

To give the tree a good start in the year, you should let the first spring shoots grow relatively long — about 8 in (20 cm) on younger plants and 6 in (15 cm) on older trees — before cutting back hard. After about a fortnight of new growth, you can then prune shoots that have only grown to 4 cm (10 cm). This strategy will keep the outer branches thinner and more finely structured.

A ten-year-old smooth-leaved elm

Each pruning is followed by new growth, so from August onwards it's a good idea to pinch the shoots out so as to stop any further growth. As soon as a shoot develops three or four leaves, you should remove the shoot tip.

It's best to remove older branches in the early spring, before growth begins. Afterwards you should seal all the wounds carefully with a good wound sealant.

Wiring

With the smooth-leaved elm (*U. carpinifolia*) you can normally manage without wiring, as careful pruning is usually enough to make the branches grow in the right direction. With older plants it can sometimes be necessary to change the direction of existing branches. However, this can best be achieved with the help of tensioned wire.

Obtaining plants

If you want to propagate from seed, then you should collect the seed in May and sow out immediately.

You can often find young plants if you're out on a walk, or failing that at a tree nursery. Bonsai specialists offer starter plants at various stages of development. Also on sale are a variety of more mature elms and zelkovas, again at various stages, and including some fully styled specimens.

Maidenhair tree

The ginkgo, or maidenhair tree (*Ginkgo biloba*), is a true 'living fossil' — the earliest tree known to have evolved (before both conifers and flowering plants). Although it has leaves rather than needles, it is normally classified with the conifers rather than the broadleaves.

The ginkgo is dioecious — i.e. there are separate male and female plants. Once the female flowers have been pollinated, they develop into evil-smelling, plum-like fruits that ripen to a yellow colour.

Bonsai requirements
Because the maidenhair tree is so robust and resistant to disease, it's extremely easy to look after. It likes a sunny or semi-shaded position in the open air, and tolerates most kinds of weather. In the spring, however, it may well need protection from late frosts.

The soil should contain a high proportion of granular material so that excess water can drain away properly; the roots rot very easily if the soil is kept too moist. With young plants, most of the soil should be changed every other year, while older plants can wait up to three years; you should trim the roots at the same time.

The maidenhair tree isn't very fussy about the kind of water you use, but you should only water it when the soil surface has dried out. Feed the tree with an organic or inorganic bonsai fertiliser from the time the first leaves appear right up until the end of August.

Overwinter the plant outside its container, in a garden bed that is protected from direct sunlight. If you only have a balcony, then you should place the tree in a trough full of sand and peat substitute.

Styles
This tree is very reluctant to form branches, which makes it difficult to shape. After pruning, each shoot normally grows only a single replacement. If there are additional branches, they will usually only grow from the winter buds.

The only style that can be achieved without wiring is the broom style. Other styles will need regular wiring.

Wiring
Only branches up to the thickness of a pencil can easily be wired. Thicker branches are very rigid, and cannot generally be bent without leaving pressure marks on the bark; it's better to pull them into shape with tensioned wire.

Pruning
To encourage branching, you should cut off all the end buds in the upper part of the crown in the early spring, before growth begins. When the first shoots are about 8 in (20 cm) long, cut them back to between two and three leaves. Normally only the bud nearest the cut will actually sprout.

Larger wounds will heal only very slowly. If you need to remove a larger branch, you should do this soon after spring growth begins.

Obtaining plants
To obtain the seed, remove it from the fruit in the autumn, then overwinter it in damp sand in a cool place, and sow it out in spring. However, some of the seed will not actually germinate until the second year.

The maidenhair tree is easy to propagate from hardwood cuttings. For this you need some 2–4-in (5–10-cm) long pieces of branch without any leaves. Plant them so that only the top bud is visible above the soil surface. Once they have begun to sprout, you can treat them like any other seedling.

Bonsai specialists often have a good selection of young plants for sale. Older plants at various stages of development are among the standard items on offer at such outlets.

This 15-year-old ginkgo is only about 2 ft (60 cm) tall.

Juniper

Junipers (*Juniperus*) are a group
of highly adaptable evergreen
plants that can grow as shrubs,
bushes or small trees. The bark
varies in colour from grey to
reddish brown, and normally
tends to peel off in thin fibres.
The needles are mostly scale-
like in form.

There are separate male and
female cones. The male cones
look like small, round catkins.
The bud-like female cones are
pollinated on the wind, but
often don't ripen into the
familiar blue juniper berries
until the autumn of the
following year.

Our native common juniper
(*J. communis*) can be found
anywhere in the wild where
there isn't too much competition
from other trees and shrubs. It is
therefore common on heath-
lands and downlands. The
dwarf variety *J. c.* var. *nana*
grows high up on the Scottish
mountain slopes.

Bonsai requirements
As a bonsai, the juniper likes a
sunny, airy position. If branches
are deprived of sunlight, they
may become stunted or die off
completely.

You can water a juniper from
the tap all year round. In hot
weather it does best in damp
soil that is evenly moist, but it
can survive short periods of
dryness provided the roots are
well developed. Young plants

need plenty of feeding with an
organic fertiliser. Older, more
mature plants can be fed much
more sparingly.

All native and Japanese
junipers are very hardy. However, to keep the roots evenly
moist it's best to overwinter
them outside their containers, in
a garden bed. This is absolutely
essential with Mediterranean
species such as the hedgehog
juniper (*J. hemispherica*).

Styles
All growth habits and Japanese
styles are possible. With most
bonsai junipers, the needles
form dense cushions at the ends
of the branches.

Pruning
To keep the cushions dense,
you should prune the new
shoots when they reach about
1 in (2–3 cm) in length. Reduce
each shoot to about one-third of
its length by pinching out the
shoot tip. If a branch needs to
grow thicker, then leave the tip
shoots alone and shorten the
other shoots on the branch. This
will make the branch thicker
and create a denser cushion at
the same time.

Any larger wounds will only
heal very slowly, so the best
time to remove bigger branches
is in the spring. Treat the
wounds immediately after
pruning with a really effective
wound sealant.

This hedgehog juniper (J. hemi-spherica) is some 30 years old.

Wiring

Two-year-old branches respond best to wiring because they are strong enough without being too thick or too rigid. Juniper branches thicken only slowly, and the bark is not particularly sensitive (any scarring soon disappears when the bark peels). This means that a juniper isn't as tricky to wire as most trees. If you need to bend the branches a long way, however, it's best to do this during the main growing season and to place the tree in the shade for a few days afterwards.

Obtaining plants

Collect the ripe berries in the autumn, extract the seeds and keep them in damp sand in the refrigerator. Sow them out in the spring — but bear in mind that some of the seeds probably won't germinate until the following year.

The juniper is quite easy to propagate from cuttings taken during the summer.

Nurseries and bonsai special-ists offer a good variety of species at different stages of growth. Among the commonest on offer are various oriental imports such as the Chinese juniper (*J. chinensis*) and the needle juniper (*J. rigida*).

Larch

The European larch (*Larix decidua*) and the closely related Japanese larch (*L. kaempferi*) are both tall trees that are pyramidal in shape when grown as solitaries. The bark becomes extremely rough with age, while the branches generally become sickle-shaped.

The young shoots are yellowish brown on the European larch and reddish brown on its Japanese cousin. The needles grow singly or in clusters, and are dropped in the winter.

There are separate male and female cones. The female cones are pollinated on the wind. They are reddish-coloured at first, becoming brown and erect as they ripen. They eventually open up in October, and the winged seeds are then dispersed on the wind.

Bonsai requirements
Larches are relatively easy to care for as bonsai. They prefer a sunny position, but will also grow in semi-shade. The soil should be kept nice and moist. If it isn't, then in hot weather the tree will drop its needles. In cool weather, however, it can survive short periods of dryness without any damage.

The soil should be open and granular. A good mixture might be a combination of *akadama* or John Innes No 3 with sand and fine gravel. If you transplant infrequently and keep the soil

nutrients low, this will encourage the development of cones. Young or developing plants should be given a generous dose of organic or inorganic fertiliser as soon as the first

needles appear. Older plants, however, should be fed only very little. From July onwards, change to a low-nitrogen feed so that the tree can harden up for the autumn.

Larches are extremely frost-hardy, as one might naturally expect from the climate of their native habitats. However, if you live in a particularly cold area of the country, it may be best to

overwinter them outside their containers in a garden bed or in a trough on the balcony.

Styles

Many different styles are possible for larches, and the best ideas can generally be culled from wild plants. It's easy to bend the older branches, which means that even an older plant can be shaped without any difficulties.

Pruning

Larches are subject to the same general principle as other bonsai: the longer you allow a shoot to grow, the thicker the branch will become.

Shoots on a younger plant should be allowed to reach 4-8 in (10-20 cm) so that the branches can grow thick and strong; older plants should be pruned much earlier. With sufficient feeding, a larch shoot should regrow within two to four weeks, which is unusual for a conifer. If the branches are too dense — which can often happen at the tip of the tree — then you can cut right back into older wood.

With an older plant, provided it doesn't need to be drastically reshaped or reduced, you can simply pinch out the new shoots. When a shoot has grown to about 1 in (2-3 cm),

remove the shoot tip with tweezers or just with your fingertips. This procedure will produce a fine network of branches and twigs around the outside of the crown.

Wiring

Even older branches can be wired to shape. But if the bark on them has become rough, the wiring will leave visible marks, so it's better to pull such branches into shape with tensioned wire.

Other branches can be wired without any problems. The best time to do this is in the spring, when the leaf buds are green and ready to sprout. As larch branches thicken more quickly than those of other conifers, you should keep a close eye on the wiring. Sometimes you will need to remove it after only three months.

Obtaining plants

Collect the seed in the autumn, store it in dry conditions and sow it out in the spring

Larches between two and five years old can normally be obtained from tree nurseries. Bonsai specialists tend to sell them after they have already been shaped to some extent, so you'll often be able to style them without the need to make large wounds.

An attractive group planting of Japanese larches

Mountain pine

The mountain pine (*Pinus mugo*) comes originally from the mountain ranges of central Europe. The species is extremely variable, and botanists divide it into a whole series of sub-species and varieties. Nurseries, in their turn, have produced an even greater range of cultivated varieties. However, we shall not go into all the various forms here, as their classification is far from consistent.

The main features that distinguish the mountain pine from the more familiar Scots pine (*P. sylvestris*) are the resinous buds and the shiny-green to purplish-brown bark on the young trunk. The paired needles are 1–2 in (2–5 cm) long, dark green in colour and only slightly twisted. The cones start as bundles of violet-coloured flowers that grow in fairly large numbers along the new shoots.

Bonsai requirements
As a bonsai, the mountain pine needs a sunny spot that isn't too sheltered. It's also worth noting that any shaded branches will invariably die off.

The soil should be kept well drained but evenly moist — though the tree can tolerate being dry for short periods. Tap water is perfectly suitable for watering. The consistency of the soil should be granular, but in other respects the tree tolerates a variety of mixtures.

Young, developing plants should be fed generously from April to August. You can use a solid organic fertiliser such as Osmocote — although an inorganic feed can be used all year round. You can also vary the fertiliser to change the length of the needles: the more nitrogen in the feed, the longer they will grow.

Mountain pines are very hardy trees. But they should nonetheless be overwintered outside their containers in a garden bed. This is to ensure that the roots are kept evenly moist.

Styles
The mountain pine can be shaped to many different styles, although the broom style is perhaps somewhat inappropriate. The mountain pine is among the most popular European bonsai plants. Literati or cascade-style specimens can often be found on display at bonsai exhibitions.

Wiring
Even older branches can be wired successfully, though this isn't advisable if the bark has become rough, as the wires will then mark it. In such cases tensioned wire is generally a better option.

Mountain pines can be wired either in the winter or during the growing period. If they are wired in the winter or spring, the wires may easily become too tight by the summer. If this happens, they will cut into the bark by the autumn if you don't remove them.

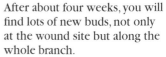

Pruning

If some time has passed since you bought your tree, and it is healthy and well developed, you can cut right back into the old wood during the first summer shaping — but you should always make sure that there are green needles on the part of the branch that remains.

After about four weeks, you will find lots of new buds, not only at the wound site but along the whole branch.

If the tree has already been styled, you should wait until July before cutting back (or completely removing) the fully developed spring shoots. If the growth has been very weak, then you can just snip off the end bud. After about four weeks, new buds will form around the wound and, to a certain extent, on parts of the branch exposed to the sun.

If you feed the plant well, there will be a new set of shoots before the summer is out — but they will remain short and produce smaller needles.

Obtaining plants

Collect the seed from ripe cones, store it in a dry place and sow out in the spring.

Tree nurseries and bonsai specialists sell many different varieties of mountain pine at different stages of development. Most specimens will tend towards a more shrubby habit, but they can be shaped as solitary trees.

If you want to take a tree from the wild, then you must first obtain the permission of the landowner. Having done so, you should lift the tree immediately after the snow has melted and before the buds start to swell.

This 30-year-old mountain pine has a most attractive habit.

73

Japanese white pine

The Japanese white pine (*Pinus parviflora*) belongs to the group of pines that have the shortest needles, and in the wild it doesn't grow very tall. The bark is tinged with grey or black, and roughens with age. The needles grow in bundles of five — hence the alternative name five-needled pine.

Each tree produces separate male and female cones, which develop on special short shoots that are often called candles. The male cones form clusters beneath the young needles; the female cones grow at the tips.

There are several well-known varieties and cultivars of the Japanese white pine.

Bonsai requirements

The Japanese have used this pine as a bonsai plant for centuries. The Japanese white pine should be kept in the open air all year round. To thrive it will need a sunny position, but it is very tolerant of wind.

Use a granular soil mixture that allows excess water to drain away. A combination of *akadama* or John Innes No 3 with sand and fine gravel should prove very successful. The soil will need changing every two or three years. The best time to do this is in the early autumn or early spring; you can prune the roots at the same time.

The inner needles turn yellow in the autumn.

The Japanese white pine benefits from the presence of this fungus (Micorrhiza).

The Japanese white pine is dependent on a fungus called *Micorrhiza*, with which it forms a symbiotic (mutually beneficial) relationship. If the soil is kept too wet, the fungus will die and the health of the tree will suffer as a consequence. For this reason, it's absolutely vital to keep the soil evenly moist at all times, and not to let it remain wet for too long.

Tap water is quite adequate for watering. The most suitable fertiliser is Osmacote or some similar organic feed. Like other conifers, this pine needs fewer feeds than a foliage tree.

Japanese white pines — and their roots, in particular — are sensitive to frost. Overwinter the tree outside its container, in a garden bed or on the balcony in a trough filled with sand and peat substitute. Cover it with straw or plastic sheeting when protection is needed from frost.

Styles

All Japanese styles are possible. However, the broom style is very unusual.

Wiring

If you want to keep your tree the right shape, then regular wiring is absolutely essential. Traditionally, this work is done in the winter.

Wire the branches almost to the tips of the long shoots, and remove all needles except those close to the branch tips. Work out how many needles to leave on the long shoots by looking at the amount of spring growth that has developed from the relevant bud. Try to arrange the tips of the long shoots so that they go together to form a single cushion. They should be turned upwards a little, because if their tips grow downwards they will tend to die off.

Even branches as thick as your finger can still be wired, though it may be safer to pull them into shape with tensioned wire.

Pruning

With the Japanese white pine, any drastic pruning is limited to the basic styling process. Once this is done, you just need to reduce the new short shoots (candles). If there are more than two candles at the end of a long shoot, then remove the longest completely. Before the needles emerge from their sheaths, reduce the larger candles to the length of the shorter ones. If the tree is not developing branches, or has been fed over-generously, all the candles will be too long. In this case reduce them to $\frac{1}{2}$-1 in (1-2 cm). Be sure to leave some needles on candles bearing flowers. If only flowers are left, the long shoot dies off.

Obtaining plants

The seed is sometimes available from bonsai specialists. Sow it out in the spring according to the instructions on the packet.

Tree nurseries and bonsai specialists offer a range of older specimens. They vary enormously in quality, and most have been grafted onto other pine species. Fully styled bonsai plants are imported from Japan, and are available from bonsai outlets at all times of the year.

A 20-year-old Japanese white pine

Fukien tea

The Fukien tea (*Ehretia buxifolia*) is an evergreen tree named after the southeastern Chinese province of Fukien (Fujian) where it mainly originates. The small dark-green leaves are shiny and covered with hairs, providing an attractive contrast with the light-coloured, irregularly patterned bark. The small white flowers measure only a few millimetres across. They eventually develop into berries that are black when they have ripened.

The closely related *E. acuminata* comes from the nearby island of Taiwan, and is also available in bonsai form. Its leaves are larger and therefore less appropriate, but it is more robust than the Fukien tea.

Bonsai requirements

Though frequently available as a bonsai plant, the Fukien tea is not exactly easy to look after, so it isn't really suitable for beginners, who really lack the necessary experience.

The Fukien tea needs to be kept at temperatures above 54°F (12°C) all year round. This is normally possible indoors. However, the plant doesn't like dry air, so you will need to raise the humidity level by placing the container on top of a tray filled with gravel and water, always making sure the bonsai container is never in direct contact with the water. The

The flower of the Fukien tea

continuous supply of water vapour will give the plant the humidity it requires.

In the summer you can move the tree out of doors. It prefers a semi-shaded position, but don't rush things — give the plant a chance to adapt gradually to direct sunlight.

Keep the plant evenly moist, as the roots can't stand being dry. Use rain water, or failing that tap water that has been left to stand for some time.

The first thing you must do after buying a plant is to replace about one-third of the soil. The best medium to use at this stage is pure Japanese loam granules (*akadama*) or John Innes No 3. The tree arrives from China in a pot full of pure, compacted loam, which isn't suitable for our indoor climate. But the soil shouldn't be changed all at once, as once again the plant needs to make its adjustment gradually. Later on you can go over to a 2:1:1 combination of

John Innes No 3, sand and planting compost. Spring is the best time for changing the soil. Every one, two or three years you should replace about two-thirds of the soil, carefully pruning the roots at one and the same time.

If the soil contains a lot of loam, the plant will need generous feeding. Feed it weekly during the growing season, using a suitable organic fertiliser. Otherwise you should feed it every two weeks.

Styles

The Fukien tea can be shaped to all the well-known Japanese styles. Most of the plants on sale will have been kept small and will hardly be shaped at all, so they will need some basic styling. You can do this at any time of year as long as the plant is healthy and its roots are well developed.

Wiring

Young branches can be shaped by wiring. Older branches are often too rigid to bend, though tensioned wire can sometimes be effective.

Pruning

The very rigid young shoots should be pruned when they reach a length of between 4 in (10 cm) and 8 in (20 cm), depending on the plant's age and its stage of development. Any larger wounds should be treated with a suitable wound sealant in order to speed up the healing process.

Obtaining plants

Wait until the fruits are black before picking them, then soak them in water for a few days so that you can extract the seeds from the flesh. Sow the seed out immediately in a soil that is low in nutrients. You'll also find that the Fukien tea can be propagated quite easily and effectively by means of cuttings.

Both *Ehretia* species are normally available from bonsai specialists. Specimens of the larger-leaved *E. acuminata* are usually allowed to grow much larger than those of the smaller-leaved Fukien tea.

This 15-year-old Fukien tea is about 16 in (40 cm) tall.

Fig tree

The many species of fig (*Ficus*) come mostly from the tropical regions of the world. The edible fig (*F. carica*) is the one exception in that it thrives in a sub-tropical climate. Figs vary enormously in their growth habits: some are creeping, some shrubby, while some grow into impressive trees.

The leaves are alternately arranged, while the flowers are contained within a strange cup-like structure that later develops into the fruit — the fig proper. When a tree is cut, the wound produces a milky substance known as latex.

Among the most popular fig species to be used for bonsai are the weeping fig (*F. benjamina*), the Chinese banyan (*F. retusa*), the willow-leaved fig (*F. salicifolia*) and the sacred fig or peepul (*F. religiosa*).

A 25-year-old Chinese banyan

Bonsai requirements

Fig trees are among the few indoor bonsai that are easy both to maintain and to shape, making them the ideal choice for the beginner.

Most so-called indoor bonsai demand a lot of effort simply to keep them alive. But the majority of fig trees will readily form a strong trunk with lots of branches that can easily be modified to the shape you want. Start your bonsai hobby with a *Ficus*, and you'll be sure of many years of fun and enjoyment.

All fig trees, including the familiar edible fig, can be kept indoors all year round. They need a well-lit position protected from the midday sun. In the summer you can put them out in the garden, but you'll need to acclimatise them gradually to direct sunlight — if you don't, the leaves may very well become scorched.

In the winter most fig trees should be kept in a heated room at a temperature of 64-79°F (18-26°C). Most species can even stand being placed above the heaters themselves. The notable exception is the edible fig, which needs to be overwintered at a temperature below 50°F (10°C).

The soil should be fairly granular so that excess water can drain away properly. A mixture of equal portions of *akadama* or John Innes No 3, sand and planting compost has proved effective. If you water the tree with tap water, the soil will need to be changed once a year, preferably in the spring; the roots can be pruned at one and the same time.

Figs react very badly to water-logging. On the other hand, they cope well with dryness, so it's best not to water them until the soil surface is dry to the touch. You can use tap water as long as you leave it to stand for a while beforehand. However, if there is any salt encrustation forming around the exposed roots or the side of the contain-er, you'll need to change the s oil once a year.

During the growing season you should feed the plant generously every two weeks. Otherwise feed it at four- to six-week intervals. You can use either an organic or an inorgan-ic fertiliser for the purpose.

A 10-year-old willow-leaved fig

Styles
Most species can be shaped to any of the Japanese styles. However, the larger-leaved species should be allowed to reach an eventual size of at least 20 in (50 cm), or the leaves will be totally out of proportion.

Wiring
Branches up to the thickness of a finger can be wired, but the sensitive bark is easily scarred by the pressure of the wires. In any case, species that grow tall in the wild tend to develop so quickly that the wires become too tight after only six weeks and have to be removed. For this reason it's normally safer to pull the bigger branches into shape with tensioned wire.

Pruning
Treatment depends largely on the age and devlopment of the plant. With plants that are still relatively young, you should allow the shoots to grow much longer where you plan to have thicker branches. But in those places where you want a branch to fork without becoming too thick — towards the top of the crown, for example — you should prune the shoots when they are still short.

If your tree is fully developed, then you should wait until the fifth new leaf appears on a branch and cut back to just one or two leaves.

Larger wounds will heal more quickly if you treat them with a good wound sealant.

Obtaining plants
Fig seed is not normally avail-able in this country. However, cuttings will root quite easily, even without the help of a rooting hormone.

Young specimens of most of the suitable fig species are on sale at most garden centres. Bonsai specialists normally offer a wide range of bonsai plants at various stages of growth and development.

79

Myrtle

The common myrtle (*Myrtus communis*) is native to the Mediterranean region, where it forms a dense evergreen shrub of moderate height.

The bark on old branches is thin but knotted. The small, dark-green leaves are extremely robust. They are lance-shaped and arranged symmetrically along the reddish-brown twigs.

Each plant has separate male and female flowers. Vast numbers of white flowers appear in the summer, later turning into black berries.

Bonsai requirements

In the summer you should place your myrtle in a sunny or semi-shaded location, either indoors or in the open air.

Overwinter it in a well-lit room that's only partially heated. In the spring, wait until the last frosts are over before moving it out of doors, and give it plenty of time to accustom itself gradually to direct sunlight (which will avoid scorching).

One of the best soil mixtures to use is a 2:1:1 combination of *akadama* or John Innes No 3, sand and planting compost. However, other granular mixtures will do equally well. You need to replace half the soil every other year, pruning the roots at the same time. During the year after the soil change, the tree will tend to produce fewer flowers.

A myrtle flower

You can water the myrtle with ordinary tap water. The roots don't react well to dryness, so you'll need to water the plant a lot during the summer, and especially during periods of hot weather.

A young plant will need regular fortnightly feeding from spring right through to the autumn. Use an organic or inorganic bonsai fertiliser. Older, more developed plants will need less feeding, and if you overfeed them they won't flower properly.

Styles

All styles and growth habits are possible. The commonest Japanese styles are upright, broom and group plantings. The small leaves mean that myrtles are particularly appropriate for *mame* pots (special small containers).

Wiring

With the broom style, and perhaps even for group plantings, you can manage without needing to do any wiring. But if you want an upright style, you normally can't avoid it, because the new shoots have a strong tendency to grow upwards.

Young branches are still nicely flexible. They don't thicken very quickly, so with regular checks you should be able to avoid the wire cutting into the bark.

However, after as little as three years the branches will have become extremely brittle, and you'll need to bend them very carefully. Moreover, tensioned wire is not advisable for older branches: if you pull them too hard, you will simply tear them off the trunk.

Pruning

With young, developing plants, wait until the new shoots are 4-6 in (10-15 cm) long and cut them back to fi-2 in (1-5 cm). As the shoots regrow, you'll need to cut them back a little more each time. You'll very soon see the result: a dense crown. At regular intervals you can even cut right back into the old wood — in fact you can cut back until there are no leaves remaining on the tree! If the trunk is already thick enough, prune the plant when the new shoots are just 2 in (5 cm) long.

If you need to remove entire branches for basic styling, this can normally be done at any time of year. If you produce large wounds, they will usually heal more quickly if you treat them with a suitable wound sealant. However, if you want to create a jin (see page 24) to give the impression of an old, damaged tree, you can simply tear off a branch.

A 15-year-old myrtle

Obtaining plants

You can harvest the ripe berries in the autumn. Remove the seeds from the flesh and over-winter them in damp sand in the refrigerator. Then sow them out in the spring.

The common myrtle can also be propagated relatively easily and effectively by means of semi-ripe cuttings.

Most garden centres sell myrtles of various ages as ordinary pot plants, and these can often make good starter plants for bonsai. Besides this, most bonsai specialists offer a wide range of myrtle bonsai at various of stages of growth and development.

Olive tree

The olive (*Olea europaea*) was among the first trees to be cultivated in the Mediterranean. It is widespread throughout that region, where there are specimens many centuries old. The trunk of this evergreen tree becomes impressively gnarled and knotted with age.

The leaves are tough, varying in shape from round to lance-shaped depending on the variety. They are dark green and shiny on top, and matt green underneath.

After pollination by insects the panicles of white flowers turn into the familiar, oil-rich fruits for which the tree is named.

Bonsai requirements

As a bonsai, the olive tree needs the best-lit position you can find. In the spring, as soon as the hard frosts are over, it's best to put it out in the open air. Choose the sunniest position available, whether in the garden or on a balcony, and keep it there until the autumn. Over-winter the olive tree on a windowsill in a room that is only partially heated.

This tree can be watered with tap water, but the quantity it needs will vary a lot depending on the season. The best guideline is to feel the surface of the soil. If it's dry, then it's time to water the plant. The colder you keep it in the winter, the less water it will need.

Use a soil mixture made up of two portions of *akadama* or John Innes No 3 to one of fine gravel — though other mixtures are also possible. You should replace about two-thirds of the soil once every two or three years, whatever the age of the tree. The best time to do this is in the spring, and it's also a good idea to prune the roots at the same time.

You can use an organic feed — or an inorganic fertiliser, as long as you're careful with it. Start with fortnightly feeds in March, reducing to monthly feeds in November.

Styles

All styles and growth habits are possible, although the broom and upright styles are the commonest. You can produce a broom style with nothing more than careful pruning. For other styles you'll often have to resort to wiring or some other means of shaping.

Wiring

Wiring should be carried out with the first spring growth. Only one-year old branches can easily be wired without damaging the bark, so you should start shaping as soon as you can. Keep a careful eye on the wires during the main growth period. If they become too tight, you should take them off and wire the branches afresh.

A 20-year-old olive tree

Older branches should be pulled into shape using tensioned wire.

Pruning

With young plants you should prune the new shoots when they reach 4-6 in (10-15 cm), reducing them to between one and three leaf pairs. With more mature specimens, you should prune the new shoots when they are only 2 in (5 cm) long.

If you need to remove any larger branches for basic styling, you can do this at any season, and you can either cut them or break them off. The wounds heal more quickly during the main growth period.

Obtaining plants

Olives can easily be propagated from seed, although fresh seed isn't normally available in this country. However, they can also be propagated successfully from semi-ripe cuttings.

Tree nurseries or garden centres sometimes sell small, roughly pruned olive plants. You might also be able to find a starter plant while on holiday in the Mediterranean. Bonsai specialists provide a range of olive bonsai at various stages of development.

Pistachio and mastic tree

The mastic tree (*Pistacia lentiscus*) is widespread throughout the Mediterranean, and is closely related to the pistachio (*P. vera*) with its edible nuts. In their native regions these evergreens are often used as hedge plants, which is an indication of how well they react to pruning. Wild specimens are commonest there in coastal areas.

The trunk tends to become grey and gnarled with age, and the compound pinnate leaves are arranged alternately. The tiny flowers grow in clusters, eventually ripening into fruits, which are black in the case of the mastic tree. The fruits of the pistachio are are white, and contain the edible nut in the form of a large seed.

Bonsai requirements

These plants need a well-lit (sunny or semi-shaded) position. Once the spring frosts are over, you can bring them out into the open air, where they can remain until the first autumn frosts are expected.

In the winter you should keep them next to the window in a room that isn't heated all the time. Place the container on a tray filled with water and hydroponic granules to humidify the air around the plant.

You can use a soil mixture made up of two portions of *akadama* or John Innes No 3 to one portion of fine gravel. Other combinations can also be used, but the important thing is good drainage. You will need to replace up to two-thirds of the soil every two or three years; you should always prune the roots at the same time.

Ordinary tap water is quite suitable for watering these plants. Feed them from February through to the autumn with an organic or inorganic bonsai fertiliser; always take care to follow the dosage instructions on the packet.

Styles

Like all trees with compound leaves, the mastic and pistachio are difficult to prune into a clear shape. However, the effect will be generally less chaotic if you don't keep your bonsai too small. Any leaves that stick out too far can be shortened to a certain extent.

All growth forms and styles are possible, but the upright style is perhaps the most common.

Wiring

These trees are difficult to shape just by pruning, which means that if you want one of the classical styles you'll probably have to resort to wiring.

One-year-old branches are easy to shape by wiring. However, older branches are more brittle, so it's best to pull them into shape by means of tensioned wire.

Pruning

The main growth periods for these trees are the spring and autumn. At these times the plant regenerates within three or four weeks of pruning. Unlike with many trees, the upper branches don't tend to dominate those below them.

You can prune at any time of year. However, bigger branches should, if possible, be removed between April and June, as the wounds heal particularly fast during these months.

Prune younger, undeveloped plants when the shoots are 6–8 in (15–20 cm) long, cutting back to one or two leaves. Older bonsai can be pruned much earlier to encourage more branching. Take care to cut at least ½ in (1 cm) away from the nearest remaining leaf: if the wound is any closer, the bud inside the leaf axil may dry out.

Obtaining plants

Fresh seed is difficult if not impossible to obtain, but you can also propagate from semi-ripe cuttings.

You can occasionally find a suitable starter in the form of a pot plant at a shop or garden centre. However, you're more likely to find a young, partly styled plant on sale from a bonsai specialist.

This ten-year-old pistachio is only 8 in (20 cm) tall.

Kusamaki

The kusamaki (*Podocarpus macrophyllus*) is an Asiatic conifer; there are a number of varieties, which differ in the size and colour of the needles. The dark-green needles are individually attached, and are unusually broad and un-needle-like. The bark becomes dark-brown and irregular with age.

There are separate male and female trees. The male flowers form whorl-shaped clusters, whereas the female flowers consist of solitary cones. After wind pollination, they develop into fleshy, rather plum-like fruit with the seed attached to an opening at the top.

Bonsai requirements

The kusamaki is the only conifer that can be kept indoors all year round. The best position for it is a sunny or semi-shaded spot near a window. If you keep it indoors all the time, the kusamaki prefers winter quarters where the temperature drops below 64°F (18°C), at least during the night.

From May to September you can also keep the kusmaki in the open air, but it will need to become accustomed to direct sunlight gradually, to avoid scorching. If you keep a kusamaki in the open air, it will even stand a slight frost (minimum temperature 27°F; –3°C). This means you can keep it outdoors all year round as long as you

The fruit of the kusamaki

can find a position that is sufficiently sheltered.

You can use tap water for watering the plant. Keep the soil evenly moist. The tree can withstand short periods of dryness.

Newly imported kusamakis normally arrive planted in very loamy soil, so in the first spring after you have acquired such a plant, you should replace the soil with *akadama* or John Innes No 3. Later on you can use a different mixture, provided it is suitably porous. You should change about two-thirds of the soil every two or three years, cutting back the roots at the same time.

If your plant is still in the development stage it will need generous doses of fertiliser (organic or inorganic) from spring through to autumn. Older trees should be fed more sparingly so that the needles don't grow so long. Don't feed your tree during the winter, because you want it to stop growing during this period.

Styles

You can create any style or shape that is suitable for a conifer. The upright style is very common because it's so easy to create from a young plant. The kusamaki grows very slowly in a container, so a lot of patience is needed when shaping it.

Wiring

One- or two-year-old branches are easy to wire. Imported trees are normally wired with steel, which unfortunately tends to leave rust stains. If the thickness (and the consequent rigidity) of the branches means that stronger wire is needed, then copper is a better material.

The branches thicken very slowly, so with regular checks you should not run much risk of the wires cutting into the bark. Even so, tensioned wire is frequently used.

Pruning

Prune young plants when the new growth has reached 6–8 in (15–20 cm), cutting the shoots back to fi–2 in (1–5 cm); this will enable the branches to grow thicker. Older plants should be pruned earlier.

Where main branches have already developed side branches, you should remove all their needles. This will activate their dormant buds and produce more new growth. If you need to remove older branches for basic styling, the resulting wounds will not heal unless you treat them with a suitable wound sealant.

Obtaining plants

Extract the seeds from the flesh of the fruits, and let them over-winter in damp sand in the refrigerator. You can then sow them out in the spring.

Alternatively, you can sow immediately after extracting the seeds, then put the seed tray in a warm place so that germination can take place.

Semi-ripe cuttings will take root at any time of year, provided you always check that the soil is kept sufficiently warm.

Young kusamaki plants are regularly available as bonsai from bonsai specialists.

A six-year-old kusamaki measuring just 8 in (20 cm) in height

Pomegranate

The pomegranate (*Punica granatum*), like the olive, is among the oldest cultivated trees in the Mediterranean region. In its original Indian home the pomegranate is considered a holy tree.

The gnarled trunk is covered with dark-grey to light-brown bark, and the branches have spiny tips. The tough, symmetrically arranged leaves are either oval or lance-shaped; they are shed in winter.

The red or orange flowers are produced in large numbers at the tips of the shoots. The fruits are similar to apples in size and shape, but are covered with tough, leathery skin. The soft interior of the fruit contains many seeds surrounded by pulp, rather like skinless berries.

The dwarf pomegranate (*P. g. nana*) grows into a large bush rather than a tree and has smaller leaves, but it also flowers more profusely.

Bonsai requirements

From the spring through to the autumn, the pomegranate prefers a sunny to semi-shaded position in the open air. In fact it can cope with any kind of weather, including strong winds. However, it should never be subjected to anything more than a slight frost (minimum temperature 28°F; –2°C).

If you keep a pomegranate indoors through the summer,

A pomegranate fruit

the leaves will often remain soft and delicate, which will turn them into tempting morsels for various pests such as whitefly. At all events, the tree should receive at least a few hours of sunshine every day.

Overwinter the pomegranate on a well-lit windowsill in a cool, unheated room. If you don't want it to lose its shape, you should discourage it from growing in the winter.

A good soil mixture is a combination of *akadama* or John Innes No 3 and fine gravel. However, other mixtures are both common and usable. You need to change about two-thirds of the soil every two or three years, regardless of the age of the tree. Always do this just before the first spring shoots, and prune the roots vigorously at the same time.

Ordinary tap water is perfectly suitable for watering. The pomegranate needs enormous amounts of water during the summer, and should be watered

as soon as the soil surface is slightly dry.

Start fertilising as soon as the first spring growth appears. Apply a fortnightly dose of solid or liquid organic feed (inorganic fertiliser may also be used).

Styles

The tree's natural growth habit is such that all styles are possible. Among the commonest is the broom style, which can be achieved by careful pruning and without any wiring.

Wiring

Older branches tend to be brittle, so it's better to pull them into shape with tensioned wire. However, one- or two-year-old branches can be easily shaped by wiring. The best time for this is the early spring, when the winter buds start to sprout. The branches don't thicken very quickly, but you should still keep a regular check on the wire to avoid the risk of its damaging the bark.

Pruning

The tree will need vigorous pruning before the spring growth begins — though if you are particularly interested in the flowers, it's best to wait until they have blossomed.

With young plants, however, the emphasis should be on the basic shape of the tree. Prune the new shoots when they reach about 6 in (15 cm) in length. Think about the eventual position of the branch in the crown, and cut it accordingly.

Normally between two and five leaf pairs should remain. The subsequent new growth should appear within two or three weeks of pruning, right through until August.

A 25-year-old pomegranate tree — height 16 in (40 cm)

Obtaining plants
The seed can be obtained from freshly bought fruit, but first you'll need to soak it in water for a few days so that the seeds can be separated from the surrounding pulp. Sow them out immediately, and put the seed tray in a warm place.

Propagation from cuttings is also possible — you'll find that semi-ripe cuttings will usually root most readily.

The dwarf pomegranate is sometimes available as a pot plant from flower shops and garden centres. Otherwise, you shouldn't find it too difficult to obtain ready-styled specimens of both the dwarf and the ordinary form from a good bonsai specialist.

Sageretia

In its Asiatic homeland the sageretia (*Sageretia theezans*) is mainly shrubby in growth, and only very rarely does it grow into a small tree.

The symmetrically arranged evergreen leaves are small and oval or ovate in form, contrasting nicely with the dark-brown to fawn-coloured trunk. The bark peels off in thin flakes to produce a very attractive pattern. The tiny flowers appear in large clusters, later developing into berries that are dark blue when ripe.

Bonsai requirements
The sageretia is one of the traditional bonsai (or rather *penjin*) species of China, where for many centuries it has been used for this purpose. Imported specimens from China are often available at very affordable prices. However, if kept indoors in this country they are very vulnerable to fungal infections such as mildew, or animal pests such as whitefly.

As long as there are no frosts, it's best to keep the sageretia out of doors in an airy, semi-shaded position. Overwinter it indoors in a room that isn't always heated, or at least where the temperature will drop low enough at night.

If you have to keep the plant indoors all year round, install a fan or a small ventilator that can be programmed to come on at regular, hourly intervals. This will significantly improve the plant's chances of warding off disease and pests.

Imported sageretias normally arrive planted in a very loamy soil that isn't suitable for them in our climate. So the first spring after you purchase a sageretia, you will need to transplant it into *akadama* or John Innes No 3, and later into a 2:1:1 combination of *akadama* (or John Innes No 3), sand and planting compost. After that you'll need to change two-thirds of the soil every one or two years, cutting back the roots at the same time. The best time to do this is in the early spring.

The sageretia always needs to be kept evenly moist. You can tell when it needs watering from the state of the soil surface. If this is just dry to the touch, then it's time to water the plant. You can use tap water that has been allowed to stand, but if you do you will need to change the soil every year so as to prevent a build-up of salts.

Regular feeding is essential to maintain the plant's health. The more loam the soil contains, the more feeding the plant will need. Feed it at intervals of between two and four weeks, depending on the season. An organic fertiliser is the best option, but an inorganic feed can be used in carefully measured amounts.

Styles
The sageretia may be Chinese rather than Japanese in origin, but you can, if you wish, shape it to any of the traditional Japanese styles. In fact, almost any shape or style is perfectly possible.

Wiring

Branches up to two years old can be easily and effectively wired. Older branches are more brittle and break easily. However, even these can sometimes be pulled into shape with tensioned wire.

Pruning

Young plants can be shaped by skilful pruning and without resorting to wires. With specimens that are still in the development phase, you should prune the shoots when they grow to 4-6 in (10-15 cm),

reducing them to between one and five leaf pairs. Older, more mature plants will need to be pruned earlier.

Obtaining plants

Squash the black fruits and soak them in water for a few days. After that you will be able separate the seed from the fruit pulp without any difficulty. Sow the seed out immediately, and place the seed tray in a warm location where it can germinate without too much difficulty.

Cuttings are commonly used for propagation. Insert semi-ripe sections of twig about 2-3 in (5-7 cm) long in a suitably nutrient-free compost. Rooting hormones aren't absolutely necessary, but they do speed up the rooting process.

You will rarely be able to obtain young plants. However, older plants that have only been partly styled are often available as bonsai, sometimes in a form that is little different from their natural growth habit. You can normally find them at specialist bonsai outlets.

This five-year-old, 8-in (20-cm) high sageretia is a typical Chinese import.

Tree of a thousand stars

The tree of a thousand stars (*Serissa foetida*), also of Asiatic origin, is best known in the UK as one of a series of cultivars with variegated leaf patterns and a range of flower shades.

The narrowly oval leaves are only ½ in (1 cm) long and symmetrically arranged; in the species they are dark green. The tree is named for the profusion of tiny, star-like flowers that appear in June. They are usually white, although there is a pink cultivar. The branches are covered in a thin, fraying bark.

Bonsai requirements
The gorgeous display of flowers makes this a very popular bonsai plant, and it is often given as a present. But it is totally unsuitable for beginners. Even experienced bonsai growers can often only manage to keep a specimen going for any length of time if it is already fairly mature.

If possible, keep this plant in stable conditions throughout the year. The slightest change, and the leaves will drop. Find a well-lit position protected from midday sun. In summer this may be in the open air; but in winter keep the plant indoors, ideally in a cool greenhouse.

The soil should not be too fine-grained. A suitable mixture might be a 2:1:1 mix of *akadama* or John Innes No 3, fine gravel and planting compost. Alas, most imported specimens

arrive planted in a sticky loam that is unsuited for our climate. When the next spring comes, change at least two-thirds of the soil, trimming the roots at the same time. The plant copes better with the change if the new soil is mainly (or entirely) *akadama* or John Innes No 3. With older plants, change part of the soil every other year.

The tree of a thousand stars should be watered with rain water, or any alternative that is low in salts. Keep the soil evenly moist; if the roots dry out, the tree will shed its leaves.

Apply generous doses of an organic bonsai fertiliser from spring through to autumn. The more loam the soil contains, the more fertiliser the plant will need. Conversely, if the tree is kept fairly cool over the winter, then it will need fewer nutrients.

In winter you can increase the humidity in the air around the plant by placing the container on a tray filled with water and hydroponic granules. The plant will then be much healthier.

Styles
The tree of a thousand stars is most often grown in the upright, broom, multiple-trunk or one of the rock-planted styles. But other styles are also possible.

Wiring
Wiring is often unavoidable with this plant because new growth

is mainly directed upwards. One- or two-year-old branches can easily be wired to shape. The branches thicken relatively slowly, which means you can leave the wires on for longer than with other plants.

Older branches can be pulled into shape with tensioned wire. However, they break extremely easily, so take great care.

Pruning
The tree of a thousand stars grows vigorously, re-establishing new growth within a few weeks of every pruning. Prune young plants when new growth reaches 4–8 in (10–20 cm) in length. Older plants need to be pruned sooner than this. Cut back new growth to between one and five leaf pairs, depending on how far the plant has developed and what position the branch is to occupy within the crown.

At the basic styling stage it is possible to cut back into older wood, but any larger wounds that result should be treated with a suitable wound sealant.

Obtaining plants
Seed is difficult if not impossible to obtain, but the tree of a thousand stars is easy to propagate from cuttings. Ready-grown plants are available from bonsai specialists in all styles and at every stage of development.

The tree of a thousand stars is yet another Chinese import. This eight-year-old rock-planted specimen has grown to just 16 in (40 cm).

Chinese elm

The Chinese elm (*Ulmus parvifolia*) is one of several Asiatic elms that thrive in a subtropical climate. The specific name *parvifolia* or 'small-leaved' was given because of its unusually small, oval leaves, which are tough in texture, dark green in colour and alternately arranged. The main colour of the trunk is dark grey, and it tends to become rough with age.

Bonsai requirements

The Chinese elm is a popular indoor bonsai plant, partly on account of its toughness and resistance to disease. It can usually overcome the ravages of poor treatment, and even of pests such as spider mites, provided you notice them in time. It does, however, need plenty of sun and humidity at all times of year. Though considered tender, it will usually survive outdoors in our relatively mild winters.

This tree needs plenty of light, with some hours of sunshine every day. Even so, the midday sun through a window pane tends to be too much for it, so it's advisable to provide some temporary shade at this time of day. You can bring the tree out into the open air from the last of the spring frosts through to the autumn. Out of doors it can stand direct sunshine all day, but you will need to accustom it to this gradually. The foliage benefits from heavy rainfall and

strong winds, which help it to become tougher and more resistant. If you overwinter the Chinese elm indoors, keep it in an unheated room in the sunniest position you can find; it should grow as little as possible during the cold season.

A good soil mixture is a 2:1:1 combination of *akadama* or John Innes No 3, sand and planting compost. Other similarly porous mixtures are equally common, and will also work well. You should replace two-thirds of the soil every one to three years, giving the roots a good pruning at the same time.

Ordinary tap water can be used for watering. This tree can even stand very hard water, and its high salt tolerance also means you can use inorganic as well as organic bonsai fertilisers. Feed the plant from February through to September as often as is stipulated on the packet. A monthly feed is sufficient in the autumn and winter.

Styles

The Chinese elm can be shaped to all the known styles and growth habits. Its lush growth, and the alternate arrangement of the leaves, means it can usually be shaped by means of careful pruning, and without resorting to wiring. But if you need to alter an older plant, or if you're

shaping such a plant for the first time, then you'll will probably have to do some wiring.

Wiring

Young branches up to the thickness of a pencil can easily be wired. With thicker branches the sensitive bark is liable to be damaged by wiring, so it's advisable to pull them into shape with tensioned wire.

Pruning

Young plants that are still developing should be pruned when the new growth reaches 4 in (10 cm). Older, mature bonsai should be pruned earlier. Reduce the shoots to between one and five leaves, depending on the plant's stage of development and the position that you anticipate for the branch within the crown as a whole.

If larger branches have to be removed in the course of drastic restyling, then it's best to do this between April and July. Bigger wounds heal very much better at this time, provided they are properly sealed.

Obtaining plants

The seed is not available in this country, but the Chinese elm is easy to propagate from cuttings. Bonsai and garden centres regularly sell older plants of various ages and at various stages of development.

A 30-year-old Chinese elm with a multiple trunk

Index